Leading with Emotional Intelligence

Malcolm Higgs • Victor Dulewicz

Leading with Emotional Intelligence

Effective Change Implementation in Today's Complex Context

palgrave
macmillan

Malcolm Higgs
Southampton Business School
Southampton
United Kingdom

Victor Dulewicz
Henley Business School
Greenlands, Oxfordshire
United Kingdom

ISBN 978-3-319-32636-8   ISBN 978-3-319-32637-5   (eBook)
DOI 10.1007/978-3-319-32637-5

Library of Congress Control Number: 2016946666

Printed on acid-free paper

This Palgrave Macmillan imprint is published by Springer Nature
The registered company is Springer International Publishing AG Switzerland

Contents

List of Figures

List of Tables

1

Introduction

1 Background

There is little doubt that leadership is one of the most researched and written about topics in the study of management in organisations. So why yet another book on the topic? There are a number of reasons, why we think that it is still worth exploring the subject of leadership further. These are:

1. The current state of research into leadership is that the evidence presented in support of the myriad of models available is often inconclusive and contradictory.
2. Organisations today are facing an unprecedented level of uncertainty, volatility, complexity and ambiguity in their environment. They face increasing demands to change and adapt to rapidly shifting contexts combined with increasing pressures to perform. These challenges are not only faced by private-sector organisations, but also by those in the public sector and, indeed, even in charity and third-sector organisations

© The Editor(s) (if applicable) and the Author(s) 2016
M. Higgs, V. Dulewicz, *Leading with Emotional Intelligence*,
DOI 10.1007/978-3-319-32637-5_1

3. There is growing evidence that the much used statement the 'people are our most important resource' has moved from the rhetoric in the statements in organisations annual accounts, to a reality. Organisations that successfully engage their employees, build commitment that, in turn, leads to higher levels of performance. In order to respond to the demands of today's challenging environment. Furthermore, such organisations build a sustainable, resilient, agile and flexible way of working that supports their need to innovate change and develop to meet the demands of their stakeholders

A problem with much of the research and writing on leadership is that it represents a search for a model that explains the way in which leaders behave in order to achieve performance in a somewhat simplistic way. In essence, it appears to be a search for the 'Holy Grail'. Academic research, that acknowledges the complexity of the phenomenon of leadership, is becoming increasingly inaccessible to practitioners. It paces rigour above relevance. Therefore, there remains a need to identify a framework for thinking about leadership that recognises the complexity of the topic and combines rigour with relevance in underpinning the framework with empirical evidence.

Against this background, in this book we set out to propose a framework that is relevant to today's organisational context. In doing this we are cognisant of the dangers of adding yet another model to the large volume that already exist. All too often new models of leadership are presented premised on the previous models being wrong. However, in doing this they still suffer from the 'Holy Grail' syndrome. We are consciously trying to avoid this. In our thinking we were influenced by the work of Karl Weick on sensemaking. In his book *Sensemaking in Organisations* (Weick, 1995) he presented the following statement:

> *We are not going to discover anything new. We need to use our knowledge to make sense in the context in which we are operating.*

In line with Weick's view we will present our thinking on leadership as one that sets out to make sense of leadership in today's challenging context.

1.1   Emotional Intelligence

One of the notable developments in thinking that was seen as being relevant to organisations in seeking to engage employees and lead to effective performance was the concept of Emotional Intelligence (EI). Whist the concept was initially put forward in 1990, it was not until the publication of Daniel Goleman's book *Emotional Intelligence: Why it can Matter More than IQ* (Goleman, 1996) that it gained traction with the broader based practitioner community and indeed the general public. The view that, other things being equal, EI accounts for the difference between personal success and failure is one that captured the interest of the media, practitioners and academics. Subsequently we have seen a stream of research and writing that has examined the broader role of EI in terms of a wide range of organisational as well as individual outcomes. The level of interest seems to result from the concept arriving at a point when the view of the organisation as being managed in a totally rational manner was coming under challenge. The complexity and volatility of organisational life was giving rise to a need to see organisations as needing to balance the rational with the emotional aspects of strategy and decision making. As a result of this, the need to engage people emotionally with their work and their organisation was proposed to be an essential underpinning of effective organisational performance as we entered the twenty-first century. In the debates around EI it did not take too long before academics and writers were proposing linkages between EI and effective leadership. Indeed, Goleman together with his colleagues published a book that set forth a direct linkage between EI and leadership (Goleman, Boyatzis, & McKee, 2002).

Once again in the debate around EI and leadership the search was on for a 'silver bullet' that provided a simplistic view of the solution to a complex set of issues. Having said that, in our own research we found significant evidence of important linkages between EI and effective leadership. However, we believed that to obtain a fuller view of the requirements of effective leadership in today's complex, volatile and uncertain environment other considerations needed to be given due weight.

1.2   Development of Leadership Thinking

In this book we do not intend to explore all aspects of the way in which our thinking about leadership has developed since the early academic studies in the late 1940s. As already mentioned, a lot of thinking has focused exclusively on the leader and falls under the broad heading of 'heroic leadership'. However, more recently there has been a shift towards viewing leadership as more of a relational set of behaviours. Furthermore, the contingent nature of these relationships has raised the need to consider approaches to leadership in the context facing an organisation. More recently, this contingent view has come to the fore in relation to the implementation of change within organisations. It is now well established that the majority of changes within organisations fail to meet their objectives. In exploring reasons for this it has been argued that the style of leadership has played a major role in such change failure. Indeed Higgs and Rowland demonstrated that up to 50% of variations in change success were attributable to leadership behaviours (Higgs & Rowland, 2011).[1]

One response to trying to make sense of leadership in today's context has been the emergence of the view that leadership needs to be seen as a shared activity as complexity and volatility in the environment increases, particularly in dealing with significant and constant organisational change.

1.3   Leading with Emotional Intelligence

In considering all of the developments in leadership thinking and research over the past 50 years we have tried to make sense of the models and findings in today's context. In doing this we have brought the concept of EI into the mix. It does appear that today leaders need to blend EI with a range of cognitive competencies (e.g., critical analysis, strategic perspective), and managerial competencies in order to balance these components to meet the needs of differing change contexts. We summarise this as *leading with emotional intelligence* and suggest that:

Effective Leadership = IQ (cognitive competencies) + EQ (Emotional Intelligence) + MQ (Managerial competences)

We also propose that whilst individual leaders need to achieve the balance between these components there is also a need to consider how these need to be developed and deployed by leadership teams.

2 Structure of the Book

In the rest of this book we will develop the above themes and present our thinking in the following chapters:

* *Chapter 2. 'The Importance of Emotional Intelligence'*

In developing our argument for the importance of emotionally intelligent leadership we begin with an exploration of the concept of EI and its emergence. We argue here that this is a concept that's time has come. In exploring the emergence of EI this chapter discusses how the concept is understood and some of the common misunderstandings. In exploring the drivers of interest in EI we will point out that it is a useful concept but, by no means a 'silver bullet'.

* *Chapter 3. 'Does Emotional Intelligence Make a Difference?'*

Having explored the nature of EI this chapter explores the extent to which there is evidence that underpins the potential value of the concept. There has been much debate around the validity of EI as a distinct concept or, indeed, anything new. In order to do this the research that has shown that EI can make a difference to individuals, teams and organisations is reviewed. We explore the way in which EI impacts on a range of significant organisational outcomes ranging from performance to well-being and provide evidence that EI is a distinct concept and adds explanation of variance in important outcomes beyond that explained by personality factors. Specifically, we examine the evidence that EI plays a role in underpinning effective leadership. However, we do highlight that it is not a simple alternative to other models and frameworks that attempt to describe effective leadership. We argue that, rather, it is part of a more complex range of considerations. This lays the foundation for our arguments for the concept of *emotionally intelligent leadership*.

- *Chapter 4. 'Measuring Emotional Intelligence'*

Having established the nature, importance and validity of EI, in this chapter we explore how an individual's EI can be measured and assessed. We then explore ways in which these measures can be used within an organisational context. Whilst we argue for the importance of using established and valid measures of EI we provide a very brief initial self-assessment guide that may be of use to the reader in preparation for exploring the later chapters in the book as well as being a guide to potential implications in their work context.

- *Chapter 5. 'Can Emotional Intelligence be Developed?'*

In our initial work on EI we were eager to ensure that we were not merely developing a new label to put on individuals (in a similar way to IQ). Our research supported the view that an individual can develop their EI through a planned programme of action. In this chapter we explore this research and outline thoughts on how EI can be developed in practice. We provide specific frameworks that can help an individual plan their own development of their EI. We also consider actions that may be established within organisations to support the development of the EI of their people (particularly managers and senior leaders) in order to improve performance.

- *Chapter 6. 'Developments in Leadership Thinking'*

Given the overall focus of our book we move from considerations of EI to look at leadership. In doing this we begin by considering the context of uncertainty, volatility, complexity and ambiguity that organisations face today. We then consider how this plays an important role in framing our thinking about leadership.

Against this background, we review the way in which leadership thinking has developed over time and the strengths and weaknesses of different models. In doing this we raise the linkages between leadership and context. The dominance of the 'heroic' model of leadership is discussed along with the dangers that this model can give rise to. In general we see that, as the context is becoming more complex and volatile, there is an emergence of more relational models of leadership that focus less on the leaders and more on their role in facilitating others to perform and engaging followers with the goals of the organisation. We argue that it is in connection with this shift in thinking that EI comes into the leadership equation. However, we also argue that other factors are also important and introduce the view that, in today's context, leaders need a balance of EI with cognitive competencies (IQ) and managerial competencies (MQ). This combination provides us with the basis for arguing that today's effective leadership entails *leading with emotional intelligence*.

- *Chapter 7. 'The Leadership Context'*

Having raised the importance of considering leadership in the context in which organisations are operating, as a basis for making sense of leadership, and considering what effective leadership looks like we turn to exploring the elements of today's context. In doing this, the drivers that are creating today's context are examined along with the implications of these. The chapter explores the increasing significance of complexity in today's environment.

Having explored the broad contextual issue we then focus on a major consequence—that of organisational change. The increasing challenges of change facing organisations are examined, along with the endemic failure of change implementation. The causes of change failure are explored, and ways of reducing these are considered. This leads to a review of approaches to change management and the trend towards a move from programmatic to more engaging and emerging approaches. The role of leaders in both selecting change approaches and leading the change are discussed and thoughts on the nature of successful change leadership are proposed.

The chapter concludes by reinforcing the view that leadership needs to take account of the context and the behaviours and practices of leaders need to be adapted to deal with the differing contexts.

* *Chapter 8. 'A Model of Emotionally Intelligent Leadership'*

In the preceding chapters, we have suggested that, in today's context, there is a need for *leading with emotional intelligence*. In this chapter, we present a model of emotionally intelligent leadership. The model encompasses the elements of EI, cognitive competences (IQ) and managerial competences (MQ). Research that describes how a blend of these components is presented, showing how such a blend leads to effective performance and the building of follower commitment. The model is further explored by demonstrating linkages to the emerging schools of thought in terms of leadership that is of a more engaging and facilitating nature. A specific element of the model is that it is dynamically related to the change context in which leadership has to be exercised.

The model encompasses some 15 elements of leadership capabilities. These are described in detail and illustrate the linkages to EI. In addition to describing the research that underpins the development of the model we also discuss its application in practice within organisations.

* *Chapter 9. 'Developing Emotionally Intelligent Leadership'*

Having presented a model of *emotionally intelligent leadership* we turn, in this chapter, to considering how this can be developed at an individual level. Ideas for development are discussed and illustrated using a case study. The chapter includes a range of development guidelines and ideas. In examining the development of emotionally intelligent leadership, we highlight the important role that followers can play in this process by being involved in giving feedback to the leaders. In a sense, this mirrors the participative and engaging relational focus of leadership that is necessary in a complex and volatile context. We also highlight the significant contribution that individual coaching can make to the development of leaders.

* *Chapter 10. 'Emotionally Intelligent Leadership Teams'*

Until this point, we have focused on EI and emotionally intelligent leadership at an individual level. However, in a complex, volatile, uncertain and ambiguous context the case has been made for seeing leadership as a distributed and, importantly, shared function. This leads us to consider the concept of an emotionally intelligent leadership team. In exploring this, we consider the research into teams and the growing significance of such research applied to senior leadership teams (particularly in complex organisational contexts). We then consider research and practice in terms of considering EI at a team level. Building on this we then examine the way in which our model of *emotionally intelligent leadership* can be applied at a team level. We provide some practical guidelines that we hope will help readers to frame team development processes and illustrate their use by means of a case study.

- *Chapter 11. Emotionally Intelligent Leadership and Organisations*

In the literature on leadership, there is an increasing view that today we need to understand that leaders impact the performance of the organisation through the creation of a culture and climate that enables employees to feel engaged, and that enables employees to realise their potential and contribute to performance. In this chapter, we consider the nature of organisational culture and how it impacts on behaviours and performance throughout the organisation.

We then explore the idea that an organisation's culture can either support or impair the development and exhibition of its employees' EI. Building on this we discuss the concept of an emotionally intelligent organisational culture. We describe research that has explored this concept and present a model of an emotionally intelligent culture. We go on to describe the development of a tool to assess an organisation's emotionally intelligent culture and present research that demonstrates that emotionally intelligent organisational cultures lead to higher levels of employee commitment and reduced intentions to leave the organisation. The chapter concludes with some guidelines for leaders who wish to build an emotionally intelligent culture.

- *Chapter 12. Concluding Thoughts*

The final chapter reviews the arguments that we have presented and the benefits of leading with EI in today's complex and uncertain context. Whilst research underpinning the arguments has been presented throughout, we discuss areas for further work to develop and increase our understanding of leadership and to help us to continue to make sense of the phenomenon as the world, and organisations within it, continue to change.

3   Conclusions

Leadership is a huge area of research and writing, yet we have no clear and unambiguous picture of the universal nature of effective leadership. This is, no doubt, because the search for such an understanding is akin to the search for the 'Holy Grail'. Rather than contribute to such a search we have followed the guidance of Karl Weick and sought to make sense of leadership as a dynamic concept that is related to the context in which it is encountered. We hope that readers find this sensemaking journey thought provoking and helpful. More particularly, we hope that the book will provide readers who are leaders, or are involved in leadership development, with some practical ideas that can inform their practice. We hope that readers who are involved in research and/or teaching in the field will find the thoughts and ideas helpful and informative in framing further research into the phenomenon of leadership.

Note

1. A more detailed account of the background to the Higgs and Rowland (2011) study can be found in Rowland, D., & Higgs, M. J. (2008). *Sustaining change: Leadership that works*. Chichester: Jossey-Bass.

Bibliography

Goleman, D. (1996). *Emotional intelligence: Why it can matter more than IQ*. New York: Bantam Books.

Goleman, D., Boyatzis, R. E., & McKee, A. (2002). *Primal leadership: Realizing the power of emotional intelligence*. Boston, MA: Harvard Business School Press.

Higgs, M. J., & Rowland, D. (2011). What does it take to implement change successfully? A study of the behavior of successful change leaders. *Journal of Applied Behavioral Science, 47*(3), 309–335.
Weick, K. E. (1995). *Sensemaking in organisations.* Thousand Oaks, CA: Sage.

2

The Importance of Emotional Intelligence

1   Introduction

In considering the idea of leading with EI it is necessary to begin by considering the development of the concept of EI. During the past 15 years we have seen an enormous amount of interest in the idea of EI. The view that, other things being equal, EI accounts for the difference between personal success and failure is one that has captured the interest of the media. What captured our interest in the early years were the numerous articles in leading newspapers that attempted to explain the performance, perceptions and, indeed, peccadilloes of leading politicians in terms of their possession or lack of this 'most desirable' characteristic. One article in a famous broadsheet newspaper in 1998 argued that the problems of the former US President, Bill Clinton, were explained by his lack of EI while another article in the same paper 2 months later claimed he had high emotional quotient (EQ). It also attributed the success of the former British Prime Minister, Tony Blair, to his high level of EI whilst stating that the former Chancellor of the Exchequer, Gordon Brown, possessed very low emotional intelligence. Many would agree that the latter was borne out many years later during his premiership. Several articles in

© The Editor(s) (if applicable) and the Author(s) 2016
M. Higgs, V. Dulewicz, *Leading with Emotional Intelligence*,
DOI 10.1007/978-3-319-32637-5_2

recent years have claimed that in this millennium a different type of business leader is required: one who possesses the quality of EI.

While it is possible to attribute this phenomenon to the journalistic powers of the 'father of emotional intelligence', Daniel Goleman, this explanation is far too simplistic. In his best-selling book, *Emotional Intelligence—Why it Matters More Than IQ* (Goleman, 1996), he presented us with an established stream of research and literature that relates to the topic. However well it is constructed, the presentation of a concept needs more than 'spin' to achieve the current level of interest. The concept, its presentation and the need for both, have to coincide in order to generate such a high level of professional, academic, business and public interest. Thus, the question arises as to the circumstances that are 'conspiring' to generate the situation in which an idea is seen so widely as offering explanations for our everyday experiences.

It is the resonance between the concept of EI with our daily experience that accounts for the level of interest in its nature and measurement. Whether we are a practising manager, academic or member of the public, we can all point to clear (and often impressive) examples of situations in which one individual has all of the rationally determined characteristics that *should* predict success, but fails to realise full potential due to the lack of an 'indefinable' personal quality. In many cases we explain this in the phrase 'they may be very bright, but they don't have much common sense'. This factor appears to be supported, if not explained, through research by such eminent academics as Bahn (1979) and Belbin (Belbin, 1993; Belbin, Aston, & Mottram, 1976) who have demonstrated that the cumulative addition of intelligence (as measured by various IQ tests) fails to explain differences in individual and team performance once a threshold level has been achieved. In a broader context, Goleman has summarised research from educationalists that demonstrates that school and early academic attainments (in a broad context) are dependent on more than 'traditional' measures of intelligence.

The core proposition of the EI 'school' is that life success requires a combination of an average level of 'traditional' intelligence with above average levels of 'EI'. This proposition certainly provides a potential explanation for the findings of Bahn who demonstrated that, beyond a certain level, 'traditional' intelligence (as measured by IQ tests) tended to be counter-productive in terms of broad measures of performance. The research into intelligence as a predictor of performance has generally shown that IQ measures do not account for a large proportion of variance. There is general agreement (from the research) that only around 20–25 per cent of the variance in individual attainment and performance in a work context is explained by differences in IQ. Having said this, the explanation of such a level of variance is considerable. However, as with any indicator of success, the focus tends to switch to what predicts the unexplained, and larger, proportion of variance. There is nothing new about the limitations of IQ in predicting an adequate amount of variation in the 'performance' of individuals when assessed in a broader 'real-world' context. The antecedents of exploring a broader view of individual characteristics that account for differences in individual success go back to the 1920s. Thorndike (1920) addressed this issue and proposed a concept of 'social intelligence' that, in combination with intellectual intelligence, would account for differentiation in individual success. The elements that Thorndike included in his 'social intelligence' bear an uncanny resemblance to current thinking on EI. However, Thorndike's thinking was not developed due to the challenges surrounding the emotive nature/nurture arguments and the growth and dominance of behaviourists in the field of psychology at the time. In an educational context, the concepts of Thorndike were revisited and explored in Gardner's work and further reinforced in Goleman's drawing together of such psychologically based research and physiological developments in our understanding of the functioning of the human brain.

The reader may be forgiven for saying 'This is all very interesting, but how can it help me in my role of working within an organisational context?' Indeed, Goleman's original work, and the stream of literature that it has prompted, attempts to address this question. However, in attempting to explore the relationship between the concept of EI and organisational behaviour the focus has been primarily on the individual's progress in the organisational context. In this arena research presents us with a significant volume of anecdotal and case study data that appears to demonstrate the organisational significance of EI. In addition, in an environment in which individuals are told (as a part of the new psychological contract) to take accountability for, and ownership of, their own career management, any information that will assist with this is bound to be widely welcomed. EI provides one further, and potentially powerful, addition to the data available to individuals in such a context.

The needs of the individual within a significantly changed organisational context, may explain a degree of interest in the concept of EI, given its apparent predictive validity in terms of personal 'success'. In this context, the definition of 'success' is fairly broad and focuses on individual, rather than organisational needs. In the early twenty-first century, this focus alone would not account for the predominance that the concept has apparently achieved. While, from an organisational perspective, EI, with its focus on the individual's role in *managing* his/her own career, may align with the new version of the psychological contract and may be appealing, it is not sufficiently compelling to account for the level of corporate, as well as individual, interest in the concept. In order to understand the level of corporate interest it is necessary to reflect on the broader changes in organisational theory, new strategic paradigms and perceptions of the drivers of sustainable competitive advantage in what is widely agreed to be a more volatile, unpredictable and fiercely competitive world.

In the search for strategies that will deliver sustainable competitive advantage, many organisations have become interested in research that focuses on 'emotional' rather than 'rational' factors. This shift is epitomised by the success of the concepts proposed by Collins and Porras (2005) in their book *Built to Last* , which emphasises the enduring dominance of emotional rather than rational components of organisational 'strategy'. The concept has been accepted by many, but is seen to be challenging in moving from conceptual acceptance to practical implementation. Fig. 2.1 illustrates the need to integrate the rational and emotional aspects of strategy and its implementation in order to achieve sustained competitive advantage.

In looking at this model it is evident that much of the historic approach to developing competitive advantage, and helping managers to deliver this, has focused on the 'rational' route. The dominance of the rational focus in organisations can be traced back to the nineteenth-century sociologist Weber, who proposed rational bureaucracy as a means of ensuring that organisational decisions and actions were objective and free from

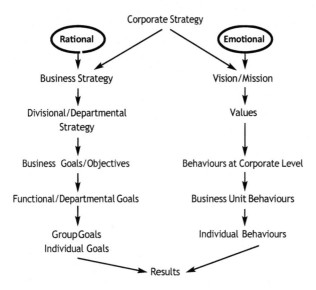

Fig. 2.1   The rational and emotional aspects of corporate strategy

emotional sway. From a managerial perspective this viewpoint became institutionalised following the work and writings of Frederick Taylor in the 1920s. He initiated the concept of 'scientific management'. These two influences have, despite many subsequent developments in management thinking and practice, ensured that rationality is deeply embedded in the organisational psyche. The 'emotional' route has traditionally been perceived as dysfunctional to organisational performance. Attempts to explore and redress the imbalance through focus on vision and values have been popular, but perceived as too 'soft' to deliver real and sustainable competitive advantage expressed through sustainable bottom-line results. Examples provided by Collins and Porras (e.g., Hewlett Packard) demonstrate the link between the rational and emotional elements of business and the value of this in delivering competitive advantage.

Another strand to the increasing focus on intangible aspects of organisational thinking and behaviour is found in the recent growth in interest in the resource-based view of strategy (Barney, 1991). This has led to an increasing focus on the value to an organisation of its human capital. The resource-based approach to strategy suggests that firms compete by exploiting their distinctive capabilities; these include the capabilities that result from highly skilled and engaged employees. This emphasis on engagement leads to a growing focus on the, so called, 'soft' elements within the organisation and again supports the emotional components of organisational life. We see the reality of the significance of engaged employees in the emergence of the 'Talent Wars', which are all about building a competitive capability in terms of human capital.

At an individual level, Goleman proposed that an average level of IQ and high level of EI is a formula for personal success. The work of Collins and Porras suggests an organisational parallel to this individual success equation (i.e., a balance between rational and emotional elements of business strategies leads to success) as shown in Fig. 2.1.

Organisations are now seeking new paradigms to help them succeed and prosper. The rhetoric of 'people provide our competitive success' has to be translated into realistic policies, practices and processes. Not only are organisations operating in increasingly volatile, competitive and global environments, they recognise that these environments are more complex. Winners in this context appear to operate in different ways. Within the UK, the success of entrepreneurial organisations such as Virgin, led by Richard Branson, have focused interest on leaders and leadership and their impact on organisational performance. The inability of research to offer consistent, valid and reliable guidance on leadership qualities and behaviours that lead to success has created a vacuum in knowledge and models that can explain and provide a basis for replicating the success of organisations such as Virgin. The concept of EI deals with perceptions of the characteristics of successful leaders such as Branson and excites interest in increasing the understanding of its reliability, nature and applicability as an organisational development tool capable of adding real value.

Most of the early literature on EI was focused on individual and 'life success'. There were a number of small studies and case descriptions that gave a tantalising view of the potential value the concept had for organisations. Over the past decade or so, prompted by the widespread interest and initial positive findings, there has been a significant growth in studies designed to examine EI in an organisational context. These studies have confirmed the relationship between EI and individual success. However, they have also shown strong relationships with individual performance, stress tolerance, morale and job satisfaction (see Chapter 5 for details). The studies have been remarkably consistent across a wide range of roles and organisational settings. Similar pictures emerge from mixed samples of managers, purchasing managers, sales staff, team leaders, air traffic controllers and even call-centre employees. Given this evidence it is clear that organisations have the potential to enhance performance either by using EI as a selection criterion or working to develop the existing employees (or, indeed, a combination of the two). The range of benefits claimed (based largely on anecdotes and small scale case histories) for focusing on EI includes:

- improved leadership;
- more effective handling and resolution of disputes;
- more effective development of team working;
- improved negotiations;
- more cost-effective decision-making; and
- better quality problem-solving and decision-making.

This is a list of attractive potential benefits that, for many organisations, goes to the heart of their ability to achieve a sustainable competitive advantage. While we believe that the evidence for performance-related benefits is relatively strong, the evidence for other benefits on this list is still emerging. In particular, the claim for the links between EI and leadership has grown both in volume and intensity. This important area is explored in some detail later. A key issue in the debate around EI is the extent to which it is feasible to develop an individual's EI. This issue is core to our thinking about applications of the concept and is one that we explore in detail in Chapter 5.

While the early case for EI was, to a large extent, based on theoretical arguments, anecdotal and derivative evidence, the authors have conducted systematic research in a business context that supports other evidence and arguments. Chapter 3 shows the validity of the concept when predicting individual success, the potential to measure the 'trait' and the possibility of developing this important set of skills and behaviours.

1.1   General Definitions and Terminology

The literature relating to EI contains a range of terminology that can be confusing. This includes:

- Emotional intelligence
- Emotional literacy
- Emotional quotient
- Personal intelligence
- Social intelligence
- Interpersonal intelligence

In essence, a common explanation is that the authors are attempting to develop and label a concept that captures the elements of an individual's personality and behaviours that are *not* concerned primarily with the rational, analytical or intellectual domains. Martinez (1997) reflects this view in a definition of EI as:

> *an array of non-cognitive skills, capabilities and competencies that influence a person's ability to cope with environmental demands and pressures.*

This definition may appeal to psychologists and other academics but it needs to be 'unpacked' to ascertain its practical meaning. Daniel Goleman who has done so much to bring the concept to the attention of a wider public, has provided a very useful initial framework for understanding what is meant by EI. In a conference presentation in 1997 he commented that EI is about:

- Knowing what you are feeling and being able to handle those feelings without having them swamp you;
- Being able to motivate yourself to get jobs done, be creative and perform at your peak; and
- Sensing what others are feeling, and handling relationships effectively.

This summary is the starting point in our explanation of the concept. We will explore this, and other views, before presenting our own definition at the end of this chapter.

In attempting to understand EI as a concept and consider how it might be of value in a business environment three important questions need to be answered. These are:

- What is emotional intelligence?
- Can it be measured?
- Can it be developed?

To a large extent these three questions have been highlighted in existing literature. However, they have not as yet been brought together in a way that helps the practitioner evaluate the value of the concept in a work context. The three questions can be seen as being closely interwoven with the measurement and development flowing from the definition and being interactive. This relationship is summarised in Fig. 2.2 with the key terminology being:

- *Emotional Intelligence.* This term refers to the overall concept as defined by Martinez (1997) and encompasses the concepts of Social Intelligence, Interpersonal Intelligence and Personal Intelligence.
- *Emotional Literacy.* This is used either as a synonym for EI or as a process involved in developing it. However, it makes more sense as a term to describe the development of EI.
- *Emotional Quotient.* This is an alternative to EI. It is more commonly used to describe an individual's EI. In much of the literature EQ is positioned as being analogous to the common measure of 'rational intelligence', IQ

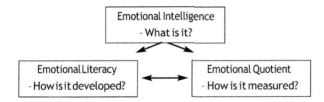

Fig. 2.2 Dynamics of emotional intelligence

2   Building an Understanding

Attempts to describe and understand any aspect of personality or behaviour are bedevilled with broad definitions that are capable of very different interpretations. To be useful within an organisational context, the concept has to be taken to a level of detail that will assist in consistent interpretation, and assist in formulating ways of measuring and developing it.

Building an understanding of the full nature of EI requires spending a little time reflecting on the background to the concept. The roots of the development of the concept of EI appear to lie in the apparent inability of measures of 'rational thinking', for example, IQ, Standard Attainment Test (SAT) scores, grades, to predict individual success in life. Goleman (1997) maintains that, in general terms, research indicates that IQ at best contributes about 20 per cent of the factors. This is certainly in line with conclusions drawn by researchers who have a *prima facie* commitment to the primacy of IQ. For example, Hernstein and Murray (1994) in a study of the relationship between IQ and 'broad' measures of life success concluded:

> *The link between test scores and those (broad) achievements is dwarfed by the totality of other characteristics which are brought to life.*

In an organisational, rather than educational, setting, Bahn (1979) reported a study that was designed to assess the validity of IQ tests in predicting executive or management competency. He concluded that leaders tended to be more intelligent than the average group member, but were not the most intelligent. His review of the studies in this field indicated a certain minimum baseline IQ as being necessary for effective performance. However, he comments that

> *If we use intelligence test scores as simply one of several indicators of competency, they can make a valuable contribution to the critically important assessments involved in executive selection and promotion. Test scores do not constitute comprehensive or final judgements about a person's capacity …. An outstanding executive is much more than a highly intelligent individual.*

The search for characteristics other than IQ, which adequately explain variations in success, is by no means new. In the 1920s, Thorndike (1920) developed the concept of social intelligence as a means of explaining variations in outcome measures not accounted for by IQ. This early venture into the field of EI was somewhat stifled by the predominance of the behaviourists in the 1920s and 1930s and the subsequent focus on cognitive psychology. The interest in a broader view of the totality of intelligence was resurrected by researchers such as Gardner and Hatch (1989). They developed and explored the concept of multiple intelligences. The spectrum of intelligences proposed by Gardner was examined in conjunction with a measure of IQ and no significant relationships were found. This led to a conclusion that the 'other' intelligences proposed by Gardner were a distinctly different construct from IQ.

In one study, people were asked to describe an 'intelligent person'. Among the main attributes was 'practical people skills'. One of the conclusions from this study was that practical people skills that are valued in the workplace include the type of sensitivity that enables managers to pick up tacit messages. Studies such as these reignited interest in Thorndike's social intelligence idea. Two more recent researchers, Mayer and Stevens (1994), identified that people may be grouped into three distinctive categories based on their styles and strategies for attending to and dealing with their emotions. These they suggested are:

- *Self-aware*: aware of their moods as they are experiencing them; autonomous and sure of their own boundaries; possessing a positive outlook on life; mindful and capable of managing their emotions.
- *Engulfed*: feeling swamped by their own emotions and helpless in terms of escaping from them; moods and emotions take charge of behaviour; unaware of their feelings with little control over their emotional lives.
- *Accepting*: having clarity about their own feelings; accepting of their moods and unmotivated or unwilling to try to change them.

An example of such additional emotional abilities is that of *empathy*. Evidence supports the view that those people who have well-developed empathy tend to be emotionally better adjusted, more sensitive, more popular and more outgoing.

Given the range of literature that explores EI, it is important for both measurement and development purposes, to develop a detailed picture of the concept, built on common elements in the literature. We have identified the core, common, components of EI. We will begin by examining these elements in more detail before describing the components of our model of EI later in this chapter.

2.1 Self-awareness

Self-awareness relates to an individual's self-knowledge. This encompasses the individual's tendency to know and be in touch with their feelings and to understand their feelings and emotions. Highly self-aware individuals tend to recognise feelings as they happen and relate their personal feelings to the context in which they are working. Self-awareness also allows individuals to make a realistic appraisal of their own strengths and thus they are able to make the most of them. They can use these feelings with confidence in a *decision-making context*.

2.2 Emotional Management and Resilience

This is an awareness of one's own feelings and emotions balanced with an ability to avoid becoming 'swamped' by them. In other words even when aware of personal feelings of cynicism or frustration, in a work context, one can still make effective decisions and fulfil responsibilities. This needs an ability to maintain a focus on results or actions while also being able to express personal feelings effectively. This component of EI needs the ability to recognise both the positive and negative impact of one's own feelings and emotions in a work context and to control these in a way that ensures both organisational and personal goals are satisfied—the ability to perform an emotional balancing act between feelings and results.

2.3   Self-motivation

Within the various descriptions of EI a strong common element relating to personal motivation arises. Daniel Goleman illustrates this by applying the concept of 'flow' to major athletes performing at their peak. This draws together ideas about what success will look and feel like together with sustained preparation, both physically and mentally, for achieving this goal. To this 'mind-set' is added a degree of self-confidence and self-belief that is grounded in a realistic appraisal of past performance. The concept is also associated with the related ideas of drive, energy and the desire to make an impact. This implies a need to balance short-term results with longer-term aspirations and an ability to pursue challenging goals in the face of short-term rejection or challenge.

2.4   Empathising with Others

This, together with managing relationships with others, would seem to be the 'soft and cuddly' elements of EI that are emphasised in media coverage of the concept. However, empathising with others does not mean being indiscriminately nice to others, nor sacrificing one's own needs and interests for those of others. In the context of EI this element is more akin to enlightened self-interest than sacrificial altruism. Indeed, it combines the ability to sense and understand what others are feeling with the ability to recognise how such feelings may conflict with organisational or situational requirements. Empathising with others encompasses a complex and often contradictory set of behaviours. The ability to recognise and have insight into the needs, motivations and feelings of others, to respond to these and to be able to resolve conflict between individual, group and organisational needs represents a high level of interpersonal skills and behaviours. In essence, this component of EI requires skills relating to social analysis, deal-making, conflict management, leadership and negotiation. It also requires the ability to convert conflicting and divergent views into creative energy through identifying and making the most of the strengths of others.

2.5   Managing Relationships with Others

This is a very wide-ranging category that encompasses the ability to build rapport in dealing with others, exhibit co-operative behaviours, promote social harmony and display social competencies. However, the ability to manage interpersonal relationships goes well beyond being co-operative and exhibiting social niceties. It is seen as the ability to manage relationships in order to achieve results, and thus entails the ability to persuade others to work as individuals and in teams to achieve important work-related goals. While this aspect of EI needs skills that relate to consensus building, it must balance the requirements of a task or project with the needs of the individuals engaged in the work. To a large extent, the effective management of relationships with others requires an ability to initiate relationships as well as the ability to respond appropriately and productively in the context of existing relationships. This requires the ability to build and maintain networks to deal with work goals, problems and issues.

2.6   Making Decisions in Complex Interpersonal Situations

Within the work environment, effective performance requires decision making that balances the 'hard' and objective information relating to a decision with the 'soft' information relating to the people involved in, and affected by, the decision. The ability to achieve this balance is an important aspect of EI. This requires an ability to cope with stress (particularly that arising from emotional conflict) and to maintain and deliver performance when under pressure. It also implies the need to be able to present one's own viewpoint clearly and to be open, honest and direct in discussing the issues relating to a specific problem or decision.

2.7   Conscientiousness and Integrity

This appears to encompass an individual's ability to accept personal responsibility and accountability for their actions and decisions as well as being open and transparent in their dealings with others. Integrity, in the context of EI, also encompasses the ability to display a high level of emotional honesty. These behaviours are seen to be important in building trust in working with others. The trust is maintained by the individual's ability to honour and deliver on the commitments that they make. This may be summarised as an ability to match actions and words in a consistent and sustained manner and to behave ethically in business life.

In looking over the nature and definition of EI outlined above, it is evident that the concept encompasses a range of individual traits, values and behaviours. This would, to a large extent, align with the concept of a competence as it is often used in practice. Indeed there are clear parallels between the drivers of interest in competencies and EI, in that both concepts have been developed as an attempt to explain variations in performance that have been inadequately or incompletely addressed by alternative concepts. The drivers for the focus on competencies are often associated with the debatable limitations on the research evidence for a link between personality and job performance. There is, within the literature on EI, frequent reference to the nature of the concept being linked to competencies. The way in which some authors have attempted to encapsulate EI as 'street smart' appears remarkably close to specific competency labels such as 'organisational savvy' described in the competency literature. The view that EI relates to a set of competencies is reinforced by leading authors in the field (including Daniel Goleman), who directly refer to using an understanding of the concept to assist in the improvement of workplace competency. A number of specific competency frameworks include high-performing competencies directly aligned to elements of EI. For example, Cockerill (Dulewicz, 1989) in identifying high-performing competencies includes a number that touch on emotions (e.g., creating a positive climate). Victor Dulewicz, in exploring and describing his 'supra-competencies', includes a grouping labelled 'interpersonal competencies', embracing: managing staff; persuasiveness; assertiveness and decisiveness; sensitivity; and oral communication (Dulewicz, 1989). Overall, the concept of EI falls within the thinking on managerial competencies. However, this relationship has not been explored in detail beyond the work described in this book and some of the more recent work carried out by Daniel Goleman. Three different types of models of EI will be described in Chapter 3.

3   The Seven Elements of Emotional Intelligence

In an attempt to pin down the precise nature of EI (Dulewicz and Higgs (2000) reviewed the literature on the concept (which is summarised above) and examined the detailed content of a range of competency frameworks. The research that underpins this categorisation, and a more detailed exploration of the elements, are dealt with in Chapter 5. They identified that the elements contained within the overall concept of EI could be grouped and defined in behavioural terms under the following seven headings (which are broadly similar to those outlined above):

3.1   Self-awareness

The awareness of one's own feelings and the capability to recognise and manage these feelings in a way which one feels that one can control. This factor includes a degree of self-belief in one's capability to manage one's emotions and to control their impact in a work environment.

3.2   Emotional Resilience

The capability to perform consistently in a range of situations under pressure and to adapt behaviour appropriately. The capability to balance the needs of the situation and task with the needs and concerns of the individuals involved. The capability to retain focus on a course of action or need for results in the face of personal challenge or criticism.

3.3   Motivation

The drive and energy to achieve clear results and make an impact and, also, to balance both short- and long-term goals with a capability to pursue demanding goals in the face of rejection or questioning.

3.4   Interpersonal Sensitivity

The ability to be aware of, and take account of, the needs and perceptions of others when arriving at decisions and proposing solutions to problems and challenges. The capability to build from this awareness and achieve the commitment of others to decisions and action ideas. The willingness to keep open one's thoughts on possible solutions to problems and to actively listen to, and reflect on, the reactions and inputs from others.

3.5   Influence

The capability to persuade others to change a viewpoint based on the understanding of their position and the recognition of the need to listen to this perspective and provide a rationale for change.

3.6   Intuitiveness

The capability to arrive at clear decisions and drive their implementation when presented with incomplete or ambiguous information using both rational and 'emotional' or intuitive perceptions of key issues and implications.

3.7   Conscientiousness

The capability to display clear commitment to a course of action in the face of challenge and to match 'words and deeds' in encouraging others to support the chosen direction. The personal commitment to pursuing an ethical solution to a difficult business issue or problem.

Although these constitute distinct personal characteristics, an individual's score on each element is related to his/her score on the overall EI Measure. These elements are reasonably similar to those identified by Goleman described previously, but they cover the domain in a slightly different way and, most importantly, bring intuitiveness into the picture. The comparison of the two sets of elements is shown in Fig. 2.3.

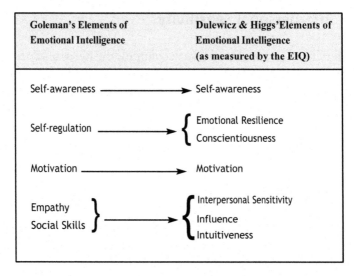

Fig. 2.3 Comparison of emotional intelligence elements

4   Tough Love

Reviewing EI on a detailed basis demonstrates very clearly that it is far more than merely becoming a warm and engaging person. The concept embraces a wide range of both 'hard' and 'soft' qualities. An individual with a well-developed EI has the ability to exercise these qualities in a continuing state of tension and balance and is able to continuously monitor and adjust this *balance* to achieve required levels of performance while still able to cope with the personal stresses and pressures this entails. In looking for a relatively simply phrase to summarise what EI is all about, the term 'tough love' seems to capture the essence of the concept. At its core there appears to be an ability to maintain a balance between compassion and caring for others with a need to meet the performance goals of a task, job or project.

Achieving this balance is a challenge. It involves working with three distinct, and potentially contradictory, groups of personal attributes and abilities. The elements of EI can be seen as falling into three categories. These are:

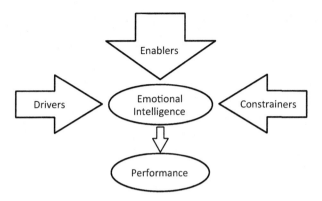

Fig. 2.4 Balance in emotional intelligence

- Drivers of performance (e.g., Motivation);
- Constrainers of actions (e.g., Integrity); and
- Facilitators of performance (e.g., Interpersonal Sensitivity, Influence).

The interrelationship between these can be summarised diagrammatically as shown in Fig. 2.4. This framework for understanding the nature and potential for developing EI is explored in more detail in Chapters 5 and 7.

To conclude this chapter, a definition of EI is needed. We have used the following from the outset:

Achieving one's goals through the ability to manage one's own feelings and emotions; to be sensitive to, and influence other key people; and to balance one's motives and drives with conscientious and ethical behaviour.

In the next chapter we will show why EI does make a difference in organisations and support this with research evidence.

Bibliography

Bahn, C. (1979). Can intelligence tests predict executive competency? *Personnel,* July–August, 52–58.

Barney, J. (1991). Firm resources and sustained competitive advantage. *Journal of Management, 17*, 99–120.

Belbin, M. (1993). *Team roles at work*. Oxford: Butterworth-Heinemann.

Belbin, R. M., Aston, B. R., & Mottram, R. D. (1976). Building effective management teams. *Journal of General Management, 3*(3), 23–29.

Collins, J., & Porras, J. I. (2005). *Built to last: Successful habits of visionary companies*. London: Random House Business Books.

Dulewicz, V. (1989). Assessment centres as the route to competence. *Personnel Management,* November.

Dulewicz, V., & Higgs, M. J. (2000). Emotional intelligence: A review an evaluation study. *Journal of Managerial Psychology, 15*(4), 341–368.

Gardner, H., & Hatch, T. (1989). Multiple intelligences go to school. *Educational Researcher, 18*(8), 8–14.

Goleman, D. (1996). *Emotional intelligence: Why it can matter more than IQ*. New York: Bantam Books.

Herrnstein, R., & Murray, C. (1994). *The bell curve: Intelligence and class structure in American life*. New York: Free Press.

Martinez, M. (1997). The smarts that count. *HR Magazine, 42*(11), 72–78.

Mayer, J. D., & Stevens, A. A. (1994). An emerging understanding of the reflective (meta-) experience of mood. *Journal of Research in Personality, 28*(3), 351–373.

Thorndike, E. L. (1920). A constant error in psychological ratings. *Journal of Applied Psychology, 4*, 25–29.

3

Does Emotional Intelligence Make a Difference?

1   Introduction

In the previous chapter we defined EI and explained why it can be important for organisations. In this chapter we provide findings from studies using the Emotional Intelligence Questionnaire (EIQ)[1] that show that EI can make a difference in predicting/explaining job and other performance measures from different organisations. Samples were comprised of managers, team leaders, salespersons and call-centre staff in large companies, and senior civil servants and Royal Navy and Police officers. In addition, we show that EI questionnaires do add significant variance in their results when compared to those produced by personality questionnaires.

2   Design of the Emotional Intelligence Questionnaire

The EIQ was designed from an extensive survey of the literature on EI and the authors' own relevant research into personal competencies of

© The Editor(s) (if applicable) and the Author(s) 2016
M. Higgs, V. Dulewicz, *Leading with Emotional Intelligence*,
DOI 10.1007/978-3-319-32637-5_3

managers. On the basis of rigorous item analysis, we identified seven separate elements of EI. These are defined briefly below:

- *Self-awareness*: Being aware of one's feelings and being able to manage them;
- *Emotional resilience*: Being able to control one's emotions and to maintain performance when under pressure;
- *Motivation*: Having the drive and energy to attain challenging goals or targets;
- *Interpersonal sensitivity*: Showing sensitivity and empathy towards others;
- *Influence*: The ability to influence and persuade others to accept your views or proposals;
- *Intuitiveness*: The ability to make decisions, using reason and intuition when appropriate; and
- *Conscientiousness*: Being consistent in words and actions, and behaving according to prevailing ethical standards.

In view of the nature of EI, we saw the need for a 360° version of the EIQ-Managerial questionnaire.[2] The original 69 items were modified so that they could be rated by a third party. Furthermore, we found a need for a version to assess non-managerial staff and so items were modified to excise any managerial content. Self and 360° versions were constructed, called the Emotional Intelligence Questionnaire—General (population).

2.1   The Current Debate About EI

There has been a fierce debate in the literature over the past 10 years about what constitutes EI; the terminology used to describe it; the methods used to measure it; and the theoretical framing of the construct. Some treat EI as an ability and have designed tests to measure it in this way. Goleman (1996) adopted a very different view, seeing it as being competency based. He produced a model with 25 competencies, derived from a consultancy framework, which Richard Boyatzis and he later reduced empirically to

20 to form the Emotional Competencies Inventory. Others, including Reuven Bar-On (1997) and Dulewicz and Higgs (2005), took a different approach and designed questionnaires and models derived from empirical research, based on personal factors related to EI, particularly 'emotionally and socially competent behaviour'. Henceforth, we use the term 'the EI personal factors model'.

At the heart of the debate are three common criticisms about EI propounded by occupational and organisational psychologists around the world in articles, books and conference papers:

1. There are no clear, defined EI constructs.
2. There is no evidence that EI predicts job performance in organisations.
3. EI questionnaires do not add any variance/explanation to that produced by personality questionnaires (via the 'Big 5' personality factors[3]).

Two leading psychologists, Ivan Robertson and Mike Smith (2001) wrote that 'a thorough search of the scientific literature failed to provide any studies which demonstrated the criterion-related validity of EI for any specific occupational area'. Others have attempted to refute these challenges in relation to Salovey and Mayer's ability model (1990), thereby raising doubts about EI models not focused on ability and thus perpetuating the myths in relation to these. However, the eminent psychologist, Professor Ed Locke (2003), argues that all these three core weaknesses apply to all EI models. In this chapter, we will present the evidence that refutes these, specifically in relation to our own questionnaire, the EIQ.

2.2   Lack of Clear, Defined EI Elements

We assert that the seven elements of the EIQ are indeed clearly defined in behavioural terms. Titles and short definitions are provided above, and much more detailed definitions are provided by us in the LDQ user manual (see note 2) and in various papers cited here.

3   Evidence that EI can Predict or Explain Job Performance

We have evidence from four different sources that prove that EIQ is based on relevant aspects of EI and that it does indeed predict performance in both private- and public-sector organisations and other outcomes such as job satisfaction and stress. This work is reported in more detail in the following sections.

3.1   EIQ Elements

As noted, the EIQ was designed from an extensive survey of the literature from nine leading EI authorities at the time by identifying common elements across their work, as shown in Table 3.1. Since some of their work was conducted within work organisations, especially Goleman and Bar-On's, this table provides evidence of content validity within a work setting.

3.2   Job Performance in the Private Sector

The authors and others have shown that EI is related to job performance by taking the EI scores of staff in managerial, sales and other positions and correlating them with job and other performance measures taken at

Table 3.1 Elements of EIQ covered by EI experts

EI element	Goleman (1996)	Gardner and Hatch (1989)	Salovey and Mayer (1990)	Steiner (1997)	Cooper and Sawaf (1997)	Bar-On (1997)
Self-awareness	✠	✠	✠	✠	✠	✠
Emotional Resilience	✠	✠	✠	✠	✠	✠
Motivation	✠		✠		✠	✠
Interpersonal Sensitivity	✠	✠	✠	✠	✠	✠
Influence	✠	✠				✠
Intuitiveness	✠	✠				
Conscientiousness	✠				✠	

the same point in time. We conducted a study of team leaders in a pharmaceutical company, which provided an opportunity to investigate the validity of the EIQ since measures of current performance were available. The results provided clear evidence for the validity of the original self-assessed EIQ-M. The total EIQ score was highly significantly related to 'performance' measures. Furthermore, all elements apart from 'sensitivity' were significantly related to 'performance'. In particular, 'motivation' and 'influence' were highly related.

This study included the 360° version of EIQ-M, using assessments by the boss. The results provide further support, with aggregated scores being significantly correlated with 'performance'. The findings showed that the total EQ score is highly significantly related to 'performance' measures whilst on the specific elements, six of the seven were significantly related to 'performance' ('sensitivity' was again the exception).

With Mark Slaski (Higgs, Dulewicz & Slaski, 2003) we provided further evidence to support the value of EI. We used two measures, the EIQ-M and Bar-On's (1997) EQ-I (a widely used and validated US measure of EI). Scores from the questionnaires were correlated with job performance ratings on a sample of 59 middle-to-senior managers from a multinational retail company. Our results showed a significant relationship between EIQ 'total score', 'self-awareness', 'emotional resilience', 'motivation' and 'job performance'. We also found similar results for EQ-i.

In view of two positive studies on sales staff reported by Daniel Goleman, we conducted another validity study in an electrical distribution company on a sample of salespeople. They completed the EIQ, their bosses the EIQ-360°. Overall sales performance was assessed by the regional managers (their bosses' superiors) in order to avoid contamination. While only two elements, 'emotional resilience' and 'motivation', were significantly related to performance on the self-assessment, when self- and boss-assessments were combined, four elements—'self-awareness', 'resilience', 'motivation' and 'influence'—plus the overall 'EI' score were significantly related to sales performance. These results provide further evidence of validity, and from a non-managerial sample.

In further exploring non-managerial performance, Malcolm Higgs (2004) conducted a study with 300 outbound call-centre staff in three organisations. Individuals completed a self-assessed version of the EIQ-G and the organisations provided job performance ratings for the individual participants. Findings indicated statistically significant relationships between overall EI and six of the seven elements (the exception being 'influence'). Interestingly, a negative relationship found between 'intuitiveness' and 'performance' appeared somewhat strange. However, when the nature of call-centre work was considered with its lack of scope for showing intuitiveness, the authors argue that these results make sense.

3.3   Job Performance in the Public Sector

A study of Royal Navy Officers by Mike Young and Victor Dulewicz (2008) explored the relationship between 'EI', 'leadership' and 'job performance' of 261 Officers and Ratings within the Royal Navy, using the formal appraisal system, EIQ scores were correlated with these performance measures. Results showed that six of the EIQ dimensions were related to overall performance, the only exception being 'intuitiveness'.

A study of police officers in the Scottish Police Force using organisational appraisal data and the 360°-EIQ by John Hawkins (Hawkins & Dulewicz, 2007) included findings on the relationship between performance as a leader and EI. Data were gathered from bosses, peers and followers as well as from officers themselves. Annual appraisal performance data were also obtained where available. The results showed a positive relationship between EQ and 'performance in policing', using both 360° overall ratings of leadership performance and job appraisals. The most supportive findings come from the 360° performance ratings, with six of the seven elements being highly significant. 'Intuitiveness' was the only exception, with all correlations being negative.

Malcolm Higgs and Paul Aitken (2003) conducted a small exploratory study in the New Zealand Civil Service, investigating the relationship between EIQ-M and predictions of leadership potential, using ratings from a development centre that included an overall potential rating (OAR) and ratings on two sub-sets of centre-criterion competencies ('cognitive' and 'interpersonal'). They found clear and strong relationships between all assessment centre ratings and the EI elements of 'self-awareness', 'motivation', 'intuitiveness' and 'conscientiousness'. It was interesting that the EIQ 'total score' showed no significant relationship with OAR but was highly correlated with both the 'cognitive' and 'interpersonal' criterion groups on both.

Overall, the studies reported here provide strong evidence for the value of the EIQ. 'Total score' was significantly related to job performance in nine of the studies. Of the elements, 'self-awareness' was the best predictor, significant in all of the studies, followed closely by 'motivation', 'conscientiousness' and 'resilience'. The weakest were 'sensitivity', 'intuitiveness' and 'influence', but even these were significant in at least four studies.

3.4   Links to Another EI Questionnaire, Job Satisfaction and Stress

In the study we conducted on retail managers with Mark Slaski (Dulewicz, Higgs, & Slaski, 2003) the total scale scores from Bar-On's EQ-i and EIQ were intercorrelated highly statistically significant, confirming that both tests are measuring broadly the same elements of EI, thus showing construct validity. The authors went on to hypothesise that EIQ scores would be related to measures of job satisfaction and stress. We found significant correlations between EIQ and both job satisfaction and stress scales. Five elements plus Total EIQ score were significantly correlated with job satisfaction and negatively with level of stress, as predicted, thus demonstrating further construct validity.

4   Does EI add Value to Personality Data?

We conducted two studies the results of which refute the third criticism: that EI questionnaires do not add any variance to that produced by the personality questionnaires using 'the Big 5'. Most psychologists agree that the 'Big 5 Personality Factors' account for most personality data. They cover: openness to experience; conscientiousness; extraversion; agreeableness and neuroticism.

4.1   Job Performance

A sophisticated statistical technique (Hierarchical Regression) was conducted during the Royal Navy Study data, reported earlier, using the Big 5 personality scores from the Occupational Personality Questionnaire (produced by SHL). The EIQ elements were the input (independent variables) and formal Appraised Performance the output (dependent variable). Results support the hypothesis that EI factors do add statistically significant variance to that produced by the Big 5 personality factors alone. The latter explain 5 per cent of the variance/variation on the performance appraisal data but when the EIQ scores are added, they explain a further 7 per cent, a highly statistically significant addition.

4.2   Happiness and Psychological Well-Being

We assessed 150 Managers using three popular and well validated *well-being* scales: the Subjective Happiness Scale (Lyubomirsky & Lepper, 1999); the Satisfaction with Life Scale (Diener, Emmons, Larson, & Griffin, 1985); and the Meaning in Life Questionnaire [Presence] (Steger, Frazier, Oishi, & Kaler, 2006). An overall well-being scale score was derived from all 14 items, which proved to be highly reliable. In addition, data were collected on the EIQ-M and 16PF personality questionnaire from which Big 5 scores were computed. In conducting a hierarchical regression with 16PF and EIQ elements as input (independent) variables, and both 'happiness' and 'psychological well-being' as output (dependent) variables, our results provided further confirmation that EI factors add statistically significant variance to that produced by the Big 5, this time from a different personality questionnaire, the 16PF. The latter explain 12 per cent of the variance/variation on the 'happiness' data from Lyubomirsky and Lepper's scale but when the EIQ scores are added, they explain a further 7 per cent, a statistically significant addition. With 'psychological well-being', the personality data explain 9 per cent of the variance/variation on the 'performance appraisal' data but when the EIQ scores are added, they explain a further 7 per cent, again a statistically significant addition. The results of these two studies provide further evidence to refute the criticism that EI does not add anything to personality questionnaires, that is, explain significantly more variance than personality factors alone.

5   Conclusion: Support for Emotional Intelligence

We have countered much of the criticism of EI. This chapter has shown that two EI questionnaires, EIQ and EQ-i, do have clear, well-defined and valid constructs. In addition, we provide evidence that EIQ explains and predicts job performance in many different work settings, as do other '*competencies and personal factor*' questionnaires. Finally, evidence from the Royal Navy and well-being studies clearly shows that EI does add significant variance, and so explains more than that produced by personality questionnaires alone, using two different personality questionnaires. The evidence confirms that EI does make a difference for those working on personnel selection and development within organisations. In the next chapter we will describe how EI can be measured.

Notes

1. A full assessment of EI referred to in this chapter (EIQ-M) has been developed and validated by the authors and is available from VDA associates. Further development of the assessment tool was the inclusion of a 360° version (EIQ-M 360) also available from VDA Associates.
2. Further details are provided in the technical manual for the Leadership Dimensions Questionnaire published by VDA Consultants.
3. There is now wide use of the concept of the 'Big 5' personality factors. For example, see, McCrae, R. R., & Costa, P. T. Jr. (1997a). Personality trait structure as a human universal. *American Psychologist, 52,* 509–516. Also see: Costa, P. T., & McCrae, R. R. (2006). Neuroticism, somatic complaints and disease: Is the bark worse than the bite? *Journal of Personality, 55*(2), 299–316.

Bibliography

Bar-On, R. (1997). *Bar-On Emotional Quotient Inventory (EQ-i): Technical manual.* Toronto: Multi-Health Systems.

Cooper, R. K., & Sawaf, A. (1997). Executive EQ: Emotional Intelligence in leadership and organizations. New York: Grosset Putnam.

Diener, E., Emmons, R. A., Larson, R. J., & Griffin, S. (1985). The satisfaction with life scale. *Journal of Personality Assessment, 49*, 71–75.

Dulewicz, V. & Higgs, M. J. (2005). Assessing leadership styles and organisational context. Journal of Managerial Psychology, 20(2), 105–123.

Dulewicz, V., Higgs, M. J., & Slaski, M. (2003). Emotional intelligence: Content, Construct and concurrent validity. *Journal of Managerial Psychology, 18*(5), 405–420.

Gardner, H. & Hatch, T. (1989). Multiple intelligences go to school. Educational Researcher, 18(8), 8–14.

Goleman, D. (1996). *Emotional intelligence: Why it can matter more than IQ.* New York: Bantam Books.

Hawkins, J., & Dulewicz, V. (2007). The relationship between performance as a leader and emotional intelligence, intellectual competencies and managerial competencies. *Journal of General Management, 33*(2), 57–78.

Higgs, M. J. (2004). Call centre performance and emotional intelligence. *Journal of Managerial Psychology, 19*(4), 442–454.

Higgs, M. J., & Aitken, P. (2003). Is emotional intelligence a predictor of leadership potential? *Journal of Managerial Psychology, 18*(4), 814–823.

Locke, E. A. (2003). Good definitions: The epistemological foundation of scientific progress. In J. Greenberg (Ed.), *Organizational behavior: The state of the science.* Mahwah, NJ: Erlbaum.

Lyubomirsky, S., & Lepper, H. S. (1999). A measure of subjective happiness: Preliminary reliability and construct validation. *Social Indicators Research, 46*, 137–155.

Robertson, I. T., & Smith, M. (2001). Personnel selection. *Journal of Occupational and Organizational Psychology, 74*, 441–472.

Salovey, P. & Mayer, J. D. (1990). Emotional Intelligence. Imagination, Cognition and Personality, 9, 185–211.

Steiner, C. (1997). Achieving emotional literacy. London: Bloomsbury Publishing.

Steger, M. F., Frazier, P., Oishi, S., & Kaler, M. (2006). The meaning in Life questionnaire: Assessing the presence of and search for meaning in life. *Journal of Counselling Psychology, 53*(1), 80–93.

Young, M., & Dulewicz, V. (2008). Similarities and differences in the competencies of effective command, performance, leadership and management in the British Royal Navy. *British Journal of Management, 19*, 17–32.

4

Measuring Emotional Intelligence

1   Introduction

Having explored the value of EI in contributing to success at work,
it is inevitable that anyone reading this would be interested in working out their own level of EI. Hopefully such an interested reader
would recognise that this question cannot be answered by a *simple* self-
administered questionnaire. EI is a wide-ranging and complex concept
with no quick or easy indicators. The level of an individual's EI may
be assessed through a structured examination of a specific group of
competencies or through using a well-researched and developed psychometric assessment. Many readers may find this frustrating, as they
will want to know their own level of EI so that they can take action to
develop and improve their capability in this area. In particular, this may
become a more important consideration as we explore the link between
EI and leadership practice and potential in subsequent chapters. This
brief chapter has been developed to help the reader conduct a tentative
assessment of their EI to satisfy their curiosity and help them approach
the balance of the book with a number of practical questions in mind.
These can be explored further when reading Chapter 5, 'Can Emotional

© The Editor(s) (if applicable) and the Author(s) 2016   **43**
M. Higgs, V. Dulewicz, *Leading with Emotional Intelligence*,
DOI 10.1007/978-3-319-32637-5_4

Intelligence be Developed?' Should the reader require a more specific assessment before reflecting on developmental activity we have proposed a process for building a firmer foundation for their assessment. Those who seek an absolute measure of their EI should arrange to take a full psychometric assessment.

2   Making an Initial Assessment

A relatively straightforward way of making an initial assessment of your own level of EI is to reflect on the definitions of the seven component elements described in Chapter 2. For each of these elements we have outlined how you might feel or behave if you have particularly high or low levels of the element within your current repertoire of behaviours.

High level	Low level
Self-awareness	
• Aware of your feelings and emotions in a wide range of situations.	• You tend not to spend time reflecting on your feelings and are generally unaware of them in a work context.
• If you become aware of feelings or moods that disrupt your performance you attempt to control or manage them and believe it is possible to do this.	• Overall you do not believe it is feasible to manage your feelings.
• In general you have a positive outlook on life.	
Emotional resilience	
• You find it relatively easy to adjust to new situations or circumstances while at the same time focusing on your overall performance.	• If you are faced with personal criticism or challenge, you tend to find that your performance suffers.
• In general you do not find it difficult to balance the need to get a job done with the needs and concerns of those who you have to persuade to help you.	• You find it difficult to deliver consistent performance across a range of situations.
• In the face of criticism or rejection you can continue to focus on a task or your overall goals and aspirations.	• When under pressure you can become irritable or volatile.

(Continued)

High level	Low level

Motivation

- You know that you are consistently focused on results and work to overcome problems in ensuring that you attain your goals.
- You tend to set yourself challenging goals.
- You tend to set, or encourage others who work for you to set challenging goals.
- You are able to achieve high levels performance in a variety of situations.
- You believe that the potential of individuals far exceeds what is normally sought or expected in terms of contribution.

- You dislike committing to goals for yourself.
- You are unwilling or unable to encourage others to commit to challenging goals.
- You are willing to accept barriers to achieving goals without spending time and effort to challenge these barriers.
- You do not believe that either you or others working with you can achieve truly stretching objectives.

Interpersonal sensitivity

- You invest time and effort in clarifying and discussing issues with others.
- You are willing to accept the views of others or their explanations or interpretations of situations.
- You are willing to lay aside your own preferred solution when presented with a clearly better one.
- You are careful in listening to others and always check that you have understood them.
- You involve those who work for you in setting goals and objectives.

- You impose goals and objectives on others.
- Even when discussing an issue or topic you tend to ensure that your view prevails.
- You are conscious of your hierarchical relationship with others and exploit this to achieve goals you wish to achieve.

Influence

- You are effective in persuading others to accept your viewpoint on problems or issues
- In listening to others you are able to use their needs or concerns as a vehicle for changing their behaviour.
- You are successful in getting others to change their perception of a problem or situation.
- You find it relatively easy to develop rapport with others.

- You find it difficult to persuade others to accept and 'buy-in' to your ideas.
- You find that your perception of a situation and that of others rarely move closer together.
- You do not find it easy to develop rapport with others.

(continued)

(Continued)

High level	Low level
Intuitiveness	
• You are consistently able to make decisions in difficult situations and build support for these decisions.	• You are uncomfortable in making decisions unless you are certain that you have considered all angles and obtained all relevant information.
• You recognise that, in many situations, it is more important to make a decision and implement it than to have all possible information available.	• You dislike ambiguous situations.
	• You have few problems in delaying or postponing a decision until all information is available.
• You understand the complexity of business decisions and are comfortable with balancing intuitive judgement and detailed analysis.	
Conscientiousness	
• You tend to demonstrate a high level of commitment to agreed goals and methods of working.	• You are willing to compromise on your values to achieve a goal.
• You invest personal time and effort in ensuring that what you say and what you do are the same.	• There are gaps between what you say and what you do.
• You set and adhere to high personal standards of conduct.	• If you underperform you often believe it to be due to circumstances beyond your control and accept such performance.

Reflect on these elements and consider the extent to which you *consistently* exhibit behaviours at the high or low end of the scales. In making this judgement you may want to use the following assessment scale:

1. Consistently exhibit behaviours described as *low* level.
2. …
3. Exhibit behaviours that consistently lie *between the high and low level* or find that they vary between high and low level behaviours.
4. …
5. Consistently exhibit the behaviours described as *high* level.

Within this scale you can use points 2 and 4 to 'fine tune' your assessment. You could summarise your 'profile' in the format shown in Table 4.1.

Having scored yourself on the individual scales you can then decide where you might position yourself on the overall scale: for example, if

Table 4.1 Initial self-assessment

	Low		Medium		High
Scale	1	2	3	4	5
Self-awareness					
Emotional resilience					
Motivation					
Interpersonal sensitivity					
Influence					
Intuitiveness					
Conscientiousness					
Overall					

all of your ratings are medium or below, you are likely to be medium or below on the overall scale. If all ratings are medium to high then your overall rating is likely to be within this range. If your own assessments are somewhat mixed (some high or low) your overall assessment should be around the medium level.

In looking at this initial assessment and how it is made up, it becomes clear that an overall rating of EI in itself does not help with planning future development. While the overall EI level is a predictor of success, it is an understanding of the component parts that helps with planning development. Development of these elements can impact on the overall scale and thus influence the future potential to succeed. However, it is important to undertake a more structured and validated assessment of your EI before investing time and effort into development activities. Approaches to developing the elements of EI are explored in more detail in Chapter 5.

3   Refining the Assessment

The process outlined above provides a 'rough and ready' assessment of your current level and profile of EI. If you have been completely honest when making such an assessment then it can be a helpful starting point in building your capabilities in this important area. However, finding out how others see you can prove to be even more valuable in establishing the 'baseline' for future development. There is a lot of value in asking others to provide you with feedback on the same basis as you used in your initial self-assessment. Using the descriptions outlined above you can ask work colleagues (your boss, peers, etc.) to give their assessment. This can be a difficult process for them, so you might like to begin by asking an individual you work with and know well to start. If there is a lot of openness, trust and confidence between you, then the assessment process can be followed by a detailed discussion that can prove to be illuminating.

Getting feedback from one individual and contrasting the two perceptions (yours and theirs) can be very helpful. Receiving input from a range of people who may have worked with you in differing situations and relationships is even more valuable. Analysis of a range of viewpoints will give you a much clearer picture of your overall level of EI and identify any potential areas for action.

Although the discussions with individual 'raters' can be extremely valuable, an overall 'map' of perceptions can be even more helpful. Table 4.2 illustrates the possible format of such a map. This 'map' will help you to build a picture of your development needs as it will raise a number of questions. Using Table 4.2, some of these might be:

- What makes Rater 1 so consistently positive?
- Rater 2 seems closest to my own ratings. Why?
- I seem to be more positive about my own ratings than those who gave me feedback. Why? Does it mean that I don't really understand myself or that my colleagues misinterpret my actions in a way that differs from my intentions?

Table 4.2 Assessment 'map'

Scale	Own rating	Ratings of others				Average of others
		1	**2**	**3**	**4**	
Self-awareness	3	4	3	3	3	3.25
Emotional Resilience	4	5	2	2	3	4.0
Motivation	5	5	4	2	3	3.5
Interpersonal Sensitivity	4	5	4	4	3	4.0
Influence	4	3	3	2	2	2.5
Intuitiveness	3	4	2	2	3	2.75
Conscientiousness	3	5	4	4	2	3.75
Overall	3.7	4.4	3.1	2.7	2.7	3.4

- Why do I see myself as being lower on conscientiousness than others do? Could this relate to a mismatch between my intentions and others' perceptions or a lack of clarity over my own values and beliefs?
- Although overall, those who have rated me appear to agree with my own rating, there are significant differences between myself and Raters 2 and 3. Why?

A major step in understanding your development needs would be to spend time with each 'rater' discussing the differences in perception and understanding the types of behaviour that they would associate with higher level scores.

It is important to bear in mind that an exercise of this nature is not one relating to debate around the precision of assessment or measurement—it is focused on an interactive process of trying to understand, in broad terms, where you stand now in terms of EI, and how you can improve your abilities in this significant area.

4   Broadening the Assessment

In the preceding chapters the focus has been on EI in a work or business context. To build a broader picture of perceptions of your current level of EI you might find it useful to get those who know you outside work to rate you on the scales we have already used. It can be illuminating to contrast work-based ratings with domestic/social-based ratings in order to build a broader understanding of your development needs.

5   Conclusion

This brief chapter has been designed to help the reader to identify where they are at the moment in terms of EI and hence their main development needs. It is important to state that this approach has to be treated as tentative. It is based on broad scales and the acquisition of feedback from others on these broad scales. A more structured assessment should be undertaken by those who are seriously concerned about their current level of EI in order to develop more precise development needs.

Whether having undertaken a detailed assessment from the authors' psychometric test (EIQ)[1] or using the 'rough and ready' assessment outlined in this chapter, the reader should now be in a position where he/she knows where they are, in terms of EI, and any major gaps they need to address. Chapter 5 focuses on how to approach development activities designed to build capability (or exploit potential) on each of the seven dimensions of EI previously have identified. However, an in-depth assessment of this complex area provides a much greater confidence that any development is targeted appropriately.

Note

1. See note 1 in Chapter 3 on the EIQ-M and the EIQ-M 360°.

5

Can Emotional Intelligence be Developed?

1   Introduction

In Chapters 3 and 4 we introduced an overall model examining the components of EI and their potential contribution to performance in a work context. This chapter considers the feasibility of an individual being able to develop their level of EI and potential ways of doing this.

If, as research and assertions propose, EI is a significant differentiator (given broadly equivalent levels of IQ) in terms of 'life success', individual performance, and ultimately corporate success, then the question arises as to whether EI can be developed or is it a more enduring personality trait? To an extent, this question invites a review of the elusive 'nature/nurture' argument. Indeed, in Chapter 3 we presented examples of research that demonstrate that EI adds explanatory power beyond that of personality. It is evident that EI and personality are distinct concepts, albeit that they overlap to an extent. In this chapter we are not setting out to revisit or resolve the overall nature/nurture debate, but rather focusing on the development of EI. However, some issues do arise about the stage in an individual's life at which interventions designed to build EI are most effective. Goleman (1996) comments that, while EI is amenable

© The Editor(s) (if applicable) and the Author(s) 2016
M. Higgs, V. Dulewicz, *Leading with Emotional Intelligence*,
DOI 10.1007/978-3-319-32637-5_5

to development, it is interventions during childhood that are most effective and educational research provides the most robust evidence to support such a proposition. Building from this research and extensive case studies, the value of increasing EI 'skills' during childhood is promoted. However, some doubts have been raised about the effectiveness of development action at later stages in life.

In the literature that covers EI there is a strong consensus that it is a developable trait or competency and a lot of the popular literature is devoted to describing processes or programmes designed to help individuals develop their EI. In our own research we have found clear empirical evidence that supports an argument that elements of EI can be developed. In the study by Dulewicz, Higgs, and Slaski (2003) there was evidence to support the widely held belief that EI is capable of being developed. In particular, the hypothesis that the 'Enabler' elements of EI (see our model in Chapter 8, section 4.2), can be developed after relevant training action was borne out by the improvement of scores observed after training. The two studies without a specific EI training intervention showed less strong improvements in EI scores.

The significance of the potential value of EI within an organisational context has led to a range of discussions about its role and development within a managerial learning context. Indeed many authors point out that although the core EI capabilities are developed within childhood, these are plastic and are capable of being developed and changed. Workplace experiences also have a significant impact on this shaping process—what managers learn in an organisation includes 'how to feel about what they do and learn'. The emotional dimension of the work of management is reflected through working experiences and practices.

2   Developing or Exploiting?

The authors' early model of EI has been revised, in part, to take account of the empirical findings in relation to the development of EI (for further details see Dulewicz & Higgs, 2000; Higgs & Dulewicz, 2002). This resulted in the distinction between *inter-* and *intra*-personal elements shown in a revised model, which was presented in Chapter 3. Results from two further studies provide some support for the new model.

As just noted, within the overall debate on the nature of EI, there has been considerable discussion around the issue of the extent to which EI can be developed. In broad terms there is an emerging consensus that EI can be developed, but there are differing views on the extent of development possible. We had initially thought that some elements could be more readily developed than others and proposed that 'Enablers' are more amenable to development than 'Constrainers' or 'Drivers' but our views have changed in the light of our research evidence. In an attempt to explain our research findings on EI development we developed a 'vessel' analogy in an attempt to explain why some elements appear to be more amenable to development than others, which are considered to be 'exploitable'. When thinking about development, we have suggested that a person's capacity could be seen as a vessel containing fluid. The overall capacity of some elements, we believe, can be increased through training that extends the range of an individual's skills.

This explains what we refer to as being 'developable'. At the other extreme, some elements appear to be more enduring characteristics, probably formed earlier in life and so, can be seen as vessels that are fixed in size. Therefore, experience can only increase the volume of contents within the vessel, not the size of the vessel itself—this is what we mean by 'exploiting' one's capacity. Based on our own research, we now believe that the seven elements lie on a development continuum ranging from: 'easily developable, malleable' through to 'difficult to develop', giving a rise to a need to exploit one's capacity formed earlier in life.

We have found in some studies that unusual work or other experiences have encouraged some individuals to exploit their existing capacities for 'conscientiousness' and 'intuitiveness'. In another study, in which managers received EI training, the results of retesting showed that some Enablers—'self-awareness', 'influence' and 'sensitivity' – had improved after training, as we had predicted, but so too had 'motivation' and 'resilience'. Using the vessel analogy presented above, an individual's overall capacity for 'motivation' and 'resilience' could be seen to have increased through training interventions.

Our initial view that the scores of the Drivers and Constrainers are unlikely to change over time has been supported, at least in part, by our findings. 'Intuitiveness' and' conscientiousness' did not improve after training, and so can be seen as vessels which are fixed in size—experience can only increase the volume of contents within the vessel. However, results from other studies show that . 'intuitiveness' and' conscientiousness' can be improved through experience, (e.g., team leaders, and skippers and successful crews in the Global Challenge Yacht Race, see Higgs, Dulewicz, & Cranwell-Ward, 2002). This is what 'exploiting' one's capacity means. The other two elements, 'emotional resilience' and 'motivation', which we had previously considered to be only 'Exploitable' had also shown improvements after training and so probably lie between these two extremes. An overview of development action incorporating a continuum of 'Develop–Exploit' is shown in Table 5.1. Whilst further research is needed to confirm these propositions, there is certainly support for the proposition that EI can, to a certain extent, be developed. This has implications for organisations in terms of the nature and design of development activities, which we deal with in the next section. Given the evidence that EI is related to performance, it would seem reasonable to assume that organisations would be interested in devising programmes and processes designed to develop the levels of EI of their people.

Table 5.1 EI elements: The 'Develop–Exploit' continuum

EIQ elements	Develop	<→	Exploit
Personal enablers			
Self-awareness	✠		
Emotional resilience		✠	
Intuitiveness			✠
Interpersonal enablers			
Interpersonal sensitivity	✠		
Influence	✠		
Driver			
Motivation		✠	
Constrainer			
Conscientiousness			✠

3   An Overall Development Framework

With most personal development activities it is essential to adopt a planned approach in order to be able to sustain the activity. Fig. 5.1 provides a framework for a planned approach to developing EI.

The key steps in this approach are discussed below.

3.1   Step 1: Identify My Need for Development

If you completed the brief self-assessment in Chapter 4, you have already made a start on identifying some development needs. However, this is only a tentative assessment. Before investing significant time and investment of effort we recommend that you complete a structured and validated

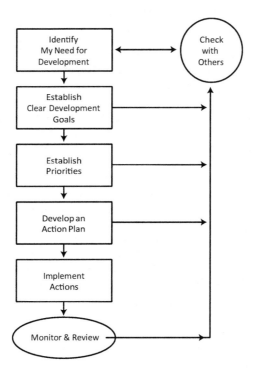

Fig. 5.1 Development framework

Table 5.2 Emotional intelligence inventory

Emotional Intelligence element	My strengths are	Examples	My weaknesses are	Examples
Self-awareness				
Emotional resilience				
Motivation				
Interpersonal sensitivity				
Influence				
Intuitiveness				
Conscientiousness				

EI assessment. Given that caveat, reflecting on your own strengths and weaknesses is a useful first step in the development process. A potential format for this is shown in Table 5.2.

To complete this inventory you should look back over the descriptions of the seven elements of EI in Chapters 2 and 3 and your earlier tentative self-assessment. No doubt, unless you are a truly exceptional person, you will be able to identify some strengths and weaknesses in relation to each of the elements. In doing this, note down specific examples of actions and behaviours that you believe demonstrate your strengths and weaknesses. To get the most from this exercise it is very important to be as honest with yourself as possible. The more specific you can be in describing examples the more helpful you will find them when it comes to later steps in the overall development process.

This is a valuable (even vital) first step, but it only represents your own view. If you have completed an assessment of EI (e.g., the EIQ: M) you can use the results as further evidence of your strengths and weaknesses. You may also have completed other personality questionnaires during your career (e.g., the Myers Briggs Type Inventory, the 16PF, or the OPQ).[1] If you have, then reviewing this information will help you in building a more accurate initial inventory. At this stage, we are focusing on developing EI in a work context. A further source of help would be notes from past job performance reviews or career review discussions.

To a large extent, EI is exhibited in your interactions with other people, so you should obtain input from other people. Spend time with others you work with (e.g., colleagues, your boss, customers) reviewing your initial draft inventory and obtaining their reactions and perceptions. This not only helps you to obtain a more accurate initial inventory, but can also be a valuable development activity in its own right. If you do not feel comfortable having such discussions with work colleagues it is important to get some form of 'independent' perspective from another person— someone who knows you well and who you can trust from outside work (a friend, relative, partner, etc.).

The need for a third-party perspective is important throughout the development process. To help to achieve this, explain the whole process to those you are talking to and try to get one or two of them to agree to act as 'guides' at later stages. Given the nature of the overall development framework at least one of these 'guides' should know you in a work context.

3.2   Step 2: Establish Clear Development Goals

Having formulated a profile of your strengths and weaknesses in terms of EI the next important step is to determine how you would like to improve. At this stage, it is worth exploring each of the elements separately. The question you should have in mind during this exploration is:

What types of behaviour would I like to be displaying in relation to this element of emotional intelligence?

Answering this question requires more than saying 'I would like to overcome all of the weaknesses'. You must develop a clear and inspiring picture of how you would really like to be in terms of actions and behaviours associated with each element. It is really helpful to be aspirational at this step. Think of what you would really like to be in terms of the elements rather than the level of improvement you feel you can comfortably achieve. Fig. 5.2 illustrates diagrammatically how we can achieve more growth by thinking aspirationally and adjusting to reality rather than thinking incrementally.

You should identify some 'role models' when developing the 'aspirational' picture for each of the elements. Identifying individuals who

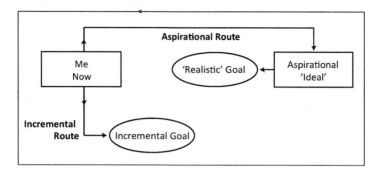

Fig. 5.2　Aspirational vs incremental

represent a really desirable set of behaviours in relation to each of the elements of EI helps to make the changes in behaviour more concrete, which you could give yourself as a target. It is unlikely that any single individual will represent a 'role model' for all seven elements of EI so you need to consider who, for you, represents a 'role model' for each element. This process of focusing on an individual is more valuable if it is someone you know, or have contact with, at work. What you are looking for at this stage is to be able to describe, in concrete terms, the actions and behaviours that you would like to be able to replicate. Although we have been focusing our discussion of EI in a work context it is possible (and perhaps desirable) to look for role models in a non-work situation. This way, we can examine the behaviours in both work and non-work contexts.

Once again the discipline of writing down your thoughts and ideas in a structured way is a valuable aid to development planning. A possible framework for this is shown in Table 5.3. Discussing your developmental goals with the 'guide(s)' you agreed to work with during Step 1 can help to ensure that you have been realistic and clear in describing the change you would like to achieve in the development process. The discussions with the 'guide(s)' are much more valuable if you are both familiar with the selected 'role models'. Failing that, you should provide your 'guide' with a vivid description of your 'role model's' behaviours and the reasons why you selected them to illustrate the element of EI you are considering.

Table 5.3 Development goals

Emotional Intelligence element	'Role model'	Behaviours the 'role model' exhibits	Behaviours that comprise my development goal
Self-awareness			
Emotional resilience			
Motivation			
Interpersonal sensitivity			
Influence			
Intuitiveness			
Conscientiousness			

When you have completed this step in the process, you should have a clear picture of 'where you are' and 'where you want to be' in terms of developing your EI.

3.3   Step 3: Establishing Priorities

On completion of Step 2, many of us are likely to be faced with a challenging agenda for personal development and change. There can be little doubt that setting out to develop EI represents a significant change initiative. To achieve success it is important that:

- you have a clear and compelling reason to change (this could either be a desire or a requirement);
- you have a clear picture of the desired end point;
- you can see and understand actions that will lead you to the desired end point; and
- you have early experience of success, which you can see moving you towards the end point.

The earlier chapters in this book, together with Steps 1 and 2, should have addressed the first two criteria. The overall development process is designed to address the third criterion (and we will return to this later). However, at the end of Step 2 we are facing a significant range of potential development needs and goals. To meet the fourth criterion, it is important to establish some development priorities. If we fail to do this then we run the risk of being 'swamped' by the magnitude of the task (unless we have outstanding emotional resilience) and will not implement our personal development and change process. One way of avoiding this is to establish an action priority list, which is likely to produce early results and which in turn will motivate us to sustain our efforts.

There are many ways in which a range of actions may be prioritised. However, in the context of change, prioritising in a way that produces early results is important in order to reinforce the commitment to change and thus sustain the effort. Fig. 5.3 illustrates a framework for prioritising actions in a change context, which is particularly helpful in planning to develop EI.

Having developed a picture of the development goals, each should be assessed and positioned on the matrix. Those which come out as a Low:Low should be reanalysed. These areas may not be related to the development of your EI or have been undervalued in terms of their difficulty or impact. Those that require considerable effort, but are likely to have little impact, are potential distracters. They could be revisited once everything else has been done, but should not be allowed to detract from the effort that you should be devoting to those areas that will have a notable impact on the development of your EI. The goals that require little effort, but are likely to have a high impact, tend to represent those areas of action where you are tempted to say 'Why on earth haven't I done something about this before?' Focus on these at an early stage. The results

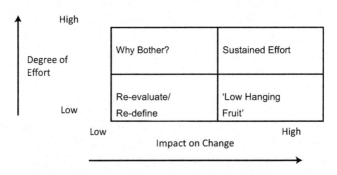

Fig. 5.3   Prioritising change

will provide you with the reinforcement and motivation required for the sustained effort to address those goals that fall into the high effort, high impact quadrant. Once again discussing and testing your own analysis with your 'guide(s)' can be of great value in ensuring that you arrive at a realistic assessment of development priorities.

3.4   Step 4: Developing an Action Plan

Once you have a clear view of your development needs and priorities it is necessary to identify the actions that you can take to underpin and realise these goals. This takes us back to the earlier questions about the relationship between the elements of EI and their developability or necessity to exploit personal characteristics. Later sections in this chapter present development prompts and ideas that may be appropriate for each of the elements of EI. However, it is worth reflecting on the general considerations that can apply to developmental and exploiting strategies. Common to both aspects is the importance of *feedback*. Whether planning to develop new behaviours or exploit (and develop strategies for coping with core aspects of your personality) it is important to begin the process by considering how you manage behavioural feedback. There are two elements to this aspect of development planning:

- learning how to use and interpret feedback from others; and
- actively seeking feedback.

In formulating an action plan it is important to build in processes and frameworks for seeking and interpreting feedback.

You should encourage regular and open feedback from others on how your behaviours are being perceived and interpreted. It is only through the perceptions of others that you are able to evaluate the effectiveness of your actions in terms of achieving your goals. Thus, any action plan you formulate should include an element that shows how you will seek and gather feedback from others. Receiving feedback is important. How you evaluate and respond to this feedback can be critical. In evaluating feedback it is critical to have an open mind. You need to look for patterns in the feedback you receive in relation to your self-perceptions. In broad terms, it is necessary to look for patterns in feedback that are derived from different sources. The greater the degree of congruence of the feedback, the more likely it is to be providing a 'true' picture of how others perceive you. Any development plans should include processes to gather, review, evaluate and respond to feedback from others.

In broad terms, if development needs relate to 'developable' components of EI then your action plan should focus on learning activities. For many of the elements that fall into these categories there are a range of interventions that are well established and readily available (e.g., training programmes focusing on negotiation skills or influencing skills). Those areas requiring 'coping' strategies that relate to the individual's personal characteristics are more difficult to plan for. While many of these areas can be addressed in the longer-term through psychoanalytic approaches there is little available that provides short-term results. In reality, people develop effective strategies for coping with personal shortcomings and playing to their strengths to counteract these. For example, intuitiveness (as an element of EI) is in the area of a personal characteristic. If an individual is low on this element a potential coping strategy may be to work on key decisions in a group or team context and to ensure that processes entail thorough risk assessment techniques with the formulation of clear up-front decision criteria. The combination of these two actions leads to a higher degree of comfort in arriving at a clear decision. From the above illustration it is clear that the 'exploitable' strategies require:

- Identification of personal areas of discomfort.
- Development of processes to examine and cover each area of discomfort.
- Achievement of a decision or action in a context different to that of discomfort.

The range of specific actions for each development goal needs to be considered in terms of:

- What has to be achieved?
- What do I need to do?

Table 5.4 Action plan

Element of EI	Development goal	Development actions	Support/ resources	Timescale
Self-awareness				
Emotional resilience				
Motivation				
Interpersonal sensitivity				
Influence				
Intuitiveness				
Conscientiousness				

- What resources/support do I need to enable me to do this?
- How long will it take to achieve meaningful results?

Developing an effective action plan is helped by formalising it and discussing it with others. A possible format for an action plan is shown in Table 5.4. Once again, considerable value can be obtained from discussing and reviewing the action plan with your 'guide(s)'. In a work context, it is important to review and discuss the action plan with those who need to support you or provide resources (particularly your immediate boss).

3.5 Stage 5: Implement Actions

This stage requires that you implement those actions to which you committed. This is the stage that requires personal commitment. The relationship you have established with your 'guide(s)' can be helpful at this stage. In developing the 'guide' relationship, it can be particularly helpful to empower your 'guide(s)' to challenge and question you or your progress in implementing your agreed actions.

3.6 Stage 6: Monitor and Review

It is very important to continue the process of self-analysis and the regular gathering and review of feedback on your actions and behaviours in order to evaluate the effectiveness of your development actions. You should actively seek feedback from all your sources to track how your development initiatives have led to real changes in your behaviours.

The feedback from this review should be used not only to check on the effectiveness of your development actions, but also to help you to formulate a further development plan.

4   Development Ideas

4.1   General Development Ideas

The nature of EI is such that it is possible to enhance the overall level by planned and sustained personal development. Much of this development will result from the individual reflecting on the behaviours you tend to exhibit in differing situations, consciously practising different behaviours and actively seeking feedback on the way in which others interpret and respond to these new behaviours.

In broad terms it is important to reflect on how the feedback might apply in a range of situations that you have faced and to recapture and reflect on these. When reviewing your feedback, and to identify development ideas, it is useful to think about a recent situation or decision and to consider the following questions:

* What were your feelings in this situation?
* How did you feel about the outcomes of your actions?
* How could the outcomes have been improved in terms of the solution of the problem/situation?
* How could the outcomes have been improved in terms of your feelings?
* What have you learned from this situation which could help you in dealing with future issues?

Within this overall approach it is important that you examine each of the EI scales and identify those where:

- you have strengths that may be developed and generalised and
- there are specific opportunities for improvement.

The following sections provide some general questions and thoughts to help you develop behaviours that will enhance your performance in relation to each of the elements of EI.

4.2   Ideas for Developing and Exploiting the Seven Elements

4.2.1   Self-awareness

In examining the self-awareness scale it is important to be reflective in terms of behaviour. You may be helped by the following prompts.
    Reflect on specific situations/problems which you have faced:

- How did you feel?
- What concerned you?
- What excited you?
- How did the reactions of others affect your feelings?
- How did you decide your actions?
- How consciously did you take account of your feelings and emotions?
- How would your responses and actions have been different if you had been aware of them?

Based on this reflection, how can you improve your reactions and solutions in the future?

4.2.2   Emotional Resilience

Thoughts and ideas which can be helpful in exploiting emotional resilience include:

- Reflect on how you adapt your behaviours to deal with different situations.

- Develop an understanding of how decisions are made and the balance between objective certainty and the need to arrive at judgements based on a balance of probabilities.
- Identify situations presenting difficult decision options and reflect on behaviours you adopted in such situations that led to successful outcomes.
- When faced with challenge spend time openly exploring the reason for it and seek opportunities to learn from such discussions.
- Actively seek opportunities to involve others in exploring solutions to difficult problems or situations.

4.2.3   Motivation

It is difficult to approach motivation in the same way as other areas of behaviour. It is important that you understand your own motivation and develop strategies to *exploit* this. The following prompts may be helpful.

- Develop a clear understanding of results and goals relating to the work situations and problems you find.
- Analyse potential for personal satisfaction and benefits that would flow from effective solution of problems.
- Reflect on situations in which you have felt a high degree of personal motivation and identify elements that may be transferred to other situations and/or generalised as work behaviours.
- Identify/build a clear picture of your personal goals/aims and establish ways in which work situations may support their achievement. Discuss your analysis with a mentor or 'uninvolved' third party.

4.2.4   Interpersonal Sensitivity

While there are a range of interventions that can be effective in building interpersonal sensitivity, it is important for you to identify actions that can be readily undertaken in a work context. Ideas to explore include:

- Spend time discussing problems and situations with team members, invite their comments and spend time reflecting on how their comments throw light on the problem.
- Make active use of a mentor to discuss work problems or situations and your interpretations of them, and of your preferred solutions on those you work with. In developing a plan or course of action, spend time reflecting on how your ideas may be perceived by those involved with or *supported* by the action.
- Reflect on situations in which you feel that you have really achieved '*buy-in*' for others and identify ways in which you can generalise the behaviours you exhibited.
- Spend time listening to others; begin by posing a problem or outlining a situation and asking for their input *before* presenting your view.

Use questions or interaction with others rather than making statements

- How much time do you spend on getting to know your co-workers and how actively do you attempt to bring their reactions to bear in understanding your own motives and actions?

4.2.5 Influence

As with interpersonal sensitivity there are a range of established development interventions or courses that can assist in building influencing skills. However, it can be helpful to use the following prompts to help you think about actions to develop your behaviours in this area.

- Spend time understanding the perspectives of others.
- Examine issues, problems and situations, and hypothesise what they might be like from the perspective of Mr X, Ms Y, etc.
- What do others need from their job, relationships with me, etc.?
- Reflect on how well I understand those I am working with.

4.2.6   Intuitiveness

Developing intuitiveness raises similar issues to those mentioned in connection with motivation. Some ideas that can help you to develop strategies to exploit your intuitiveness are:

- Develop an understanding of how you can assess and manage risks in decision making.
- Reflect on decisions that you have made in difficult situations and consider how alternative decisions may have 'played out' in practice.
- Spend time discussing complex decisions with others involved with, or impacted by, them.
- Consider how further information would have impacted on past decisions.
- When faced with difficult decisions reflect on options and potential improvements resulting from further analysis before undertaking the analysis.
- Develop an understanding of the processes of arriving at business decisions.

4.2.7   Conscientiousness

This element reflects a core trait and requires you (as with intuitiveness) to exploit your level of conscientiousness. Ideas and prompts to use in reflecting on this element include:

- Obtain feedback from others to establish the requisite level of consistency between what you say and what you do.
- Only openly commit to goals and decisions that you feel are important and can be delivered.
- Identify how others judge your commitment to decisions and actions.
- Establish a clear and rigorous approach to establishing priorities and ensure that you apply this in practice.
- Ensure that you create time to deliver your contribution to high priority actions.

The above suggestions have a strong focus on what should be examined in relation to the development of each of the seven elements of EI, but only touch on the question of 'how' very briefly. However, the development of EI is, in our view, best approached as a part of a process of personal development. In this context we feel that the keys to development relate to the willingness to undertake a sustained development process rather than seeking a 'quick fix'. This in turn requires that the individual undertaking the development is willing and motivated to change and to take ownership of the development process and its direction. The framework described earlier in the chapter, we believe, helps the individual to do this. However, if you want to undertake the development of your EI you can benefit (and indeed probably need support) from others. The areas in which you are likely to need support are:

- *Obtaining feedback*: Try to ensure that you can work with an individual whose opinions and views you trust, and explain your goals to them. Then ask them to provide you with honest and open feedback on the extent to which you are exhibiting the behaviours you seek to develop.
- *Keeping on track*: Most of us have experienced the initial enthusiasm of starting on the process of implementing a New Year's resolution. Equally most of us have relapsed. A common resolution is to lose weight, yet research suggests that fewer than 5 % of individuals who undertake a diet maintain their weight loss. This statistic changes significantly when individuals are confronted with the consequences of relapses in their plan (hence the success of organisations such as Weight Watchers and, even more significantly, Alcoholics Anonymous). The lesson from this is to set in place mechanisms to prevent relapse. Again the use of a trusted mentor or guide can help you with this.
- *Practice*: In any behaviour change process it is essential to practise new behaviours. In developing EI it is important to find a range of situations in which you can practice the targeted behaviours you want to change. Try to ensure that you select situations from which you can obtain feedback, since practice without feedback does little to help in building new behaviours.

- *Monitor and evaluate change*: Look for ways of evaluating the extent to which you have been successful in making the changes you set out to achieve. This can be by means of informal feedback or (after say six to twelve months) retaking an EI assessment to monitor the extent to which your rating on the elements you set out to change have been successful.

4.3   Is There a Course?

In working with individuals and organisations on the assessment of EI and its development we have often been confronted with questions such as:

We hear what you say about no 'quick fixes', but there must be a course we can attend to help us. Which one is it?

We genuinely cannot answer this question. The sheer popularity and high profile of the topic has spawned a myriad of courses and seminars claiming either to build EI or at least to contribute to its development. It is beyond the scope of this book (and our legal expenses insurance!) to comment on specific courses and their claims. However, it is worth emphasising that a number of the elements of EI are amenable to specific skill development that may be helped by a training course (e.g., influencing skills). However, other elements that can be developed may be assisted by broader-based training programmes. For example, the relatively recent growth in training Neuro Linguistic Programming (NLP) appears to be relevant to the development of EI. Exploring NLP training as a specific tool it is worth reflecting on a definition of NLP provided by Joseph O'Connor and John Seymour (1990).

the art and science of excellence, derived from studying how top people in different fields obtain their outstanding results.

The resonance between this definition and the view of the significance of EI as a determinant of success indicates that NLP training could be very helpful in building EI. Indeed further investigation into what NLP explores and develops shows the importance of:

- motivation;
- self-awareness;
- interpersonal sensitivity;
- emotional resilience; and
- influence.

These linkages are summarised in Table 5.5.

Although NLP training is clearly a valuable tool in developing EI it does not represent a 'quick fix'. Building NLP skills requires sustained effort to achieve personal development goals and thus may be seen as aligned to EI in its developmental philosophy.

A training 'approach' or 'model' somewhat older than NLP is that of Transactional Analysis (TA).[2] TA is built on a Freudian model of communication. At its heart, the TA model examines the breakdown of communications resulting from 'crossed transactions'. This means that one individual is engaging in a transaction in one 'mental state' while the other responds from another. The initial work on TA was carried out in the world of group therapy, by exponents such as Eric Berne and Thomas Harris. They identified that in interacting with others we use one of three 'mental states'. These they labelled as Parent, Adult and Child. The three states correspond directly to Freud's Id, Ego and Super-Ego; with Id being the Child, Ego the Adult and Super-Ego the Parent. In broad terms TA training is designed to help individuals develop effective transactions by minimising (through self-awareness and awareness of others) 'crossed transactions' and raising interactions to the

Table 5.5 NLP concepts and emotional intelligence elements

NLP concept	Emotional Intelligence element
Outcomes	Motivation, Emotional resilience
Rapport	Interpersonal sensitivity, Influence
Communication skills	Influence
Pacing and level	Influence, Interpersonal sensitivity
Doors of perception	Self-awareness

complementary Adult to Adult level. TA training addresses the EI elements of interpersonal sensitivity, self-awareness and influence. However, as with NLP, TA training requires a sustained approach to personal development rather than a 'quick fix'.

From the brief descriptions of two major established training frameworks it is evident that, while they can address a significant component of the development of EI, they also share a common view that change will result from personal development, which requires sustained effort.

5   Conclusion

By this stage we have, hopefully, shown that EI is an important factor that impacts a wide range of important outcomes in today's work context. There is evidence that it is becoming an increasingly important factor in the arena of leadership in our increasingly complex organisations.

This chapter has hopefully provided the reader with reassurance that much of EI is capable of development. Equally, it should have provided the reassurance (or possible concern!) that there is no instant transformation available through a 'quick fix' course, which people aren't telling you about. If you really are motivated to develop your EI you can do it, but you need to recognise that such a development is part of your overall development. The first step on the journey to build your EI is a genuine recognition of the need combined with the genuine desire to improve. Once you have made the first step you will be able to manage the subsequent ones.

In the next chapter we will explore the nature of leadership in today's environment and how EI becomes increasingly important as our understanding of the nature of effective leadership has developed.

Notes

1. See Chapter 3 for reference to the authors EI assessment tools. Other psychometric assessment tools referred to are:

The *MBTI*—for further details see, Myers, I. B., & McCaulley, M. H. (1989). *A guide to the development and use of the MyersBriggs type indicator*. Palo Alto, CA: Consulting Psychologists Press.
The *16 PF*—for further details see, Cattell, R. B., Eber, H. W., & Tatsuoka, M. M. (1970). *Handbook for the 16PF*. Savoy, IL: IPAT;
The *OPQ*—for further details see, Saville, P., Holdsworth, R., Nyfield, G., Cramp, L., & Mabey, W. (1993). *Occupational personality questionnaire manual*. Esher: SHL.
2. For an overview of Transactional Analysis, see, Berne, E. (1968). *Games people play*. Harmsworth, UK: Penguin Books.

Bibliography

Dulewicz, V., & Higgs, M. J. (2000). Emotional intelligence: A review an evaluation study. *Journal of Managerial Psychology, 15*(4), 341–368.

Dulewicz, V., Higgs, M. J., & Slaski, M. (2003). Emotional intelligence: Content, Construct and concurrent validity. *Journal of Managerial Psychology, 18*(5), 405–420.

Goleman, D. (1996). *Emotional intelligence: Why it can matter more than IQ*. New York: Bantam Books.

Higgs, M. J., & Dulewicz, V. (2002). *Making sense of emotional intelligence* (2nd ed.). London: ASE Test Publishing.

Higgs, M. J., Dulewicz, V., & Cranwell-Ward, J. (2002). Ocean's twelve—Leadership & team dynamics. *People Management*, 23–25.

O'Connor, J., & Seymour, J. (1990). *Introducing neuro-linguistic programming*. London: Aquarian/Thorsons.

6

Developments in Leadership Thinking

1   Introduction

In this book, we are exploring the idea that in today's context there is a need for leaders to be emotionally intelligent. Having explored the concept of EI and its validity, we now explore the way in which our thinking about leadership has developed and why EI may be required in order to lead effectively.

For centuries we have been obsessed with leaders, and with identifying the characteristics required for effective leadership. In more recent times the area of leadership has been studied more extensively than almost any other aspect of human behaviour. In spite of extensive previous research, we still seem to know little about the defining characteristics of effective leadership. However, such observations do not appear to have stemmed our appetite for continuing the search. It has been estimated that, in 2014 alone, over 1,800 books were published on the topic of leadership. Indeed, putting the search word leadership into Google will yield more than 35 million hits!

With this background in mind, this chapter sets out to explore the 'long line' of study and attempts to make sense of what we have found

© The Editor(s) (if applicable) and the Author(s) 2016   **75**
M. Higgs, V. Dulewicz, *Leading with Emotional Intelligence*,
DOI 10.1007/978-3-319-32637-5_6

in the context of today's business environment. The chapter sets out to develop a framework for thinking about leadership in terms of combining personality and behaviours. Working from this framework the possible linkages between the concepts of EI and leadership are explored with supporting empirical data.

2   Background

We have already highlighted the enormous growth in interest in the idea of EI over the past few years (Chapters 1 and 2). Over the past decade, there has been an explosive growth in the level of interest in leadership within organisations. One leading researcher pointed out that in the 1980s around 1,000 articles and academic papers were published each year in the area of leadership, but by the mid-2000s this figure had risen to somewhere in the region of 9,000! When this growth is considered alongside the huge number of books, it is clear that leadership is a 'hot topic'. What is also evident from Chapter 1 is that *not all leaders have high EI*. Given that not all leaders are really successful in the long-term it has been argued that in many organisational contexts there is a need for successful leaders to possess high EI. Given what we read about the changing nature of the business environment, this need will increase. However, in spite of the growing level of interest in leadership, we seem to be no closer to understanding what leadership is really about (Higgs, 2003).

Indeed, leadership seems to be a 'black box' or a mysterious concept. Every time an attempt is made to define what makes for effective leadership the results present us with contradictions and draw many to the conclusion that great leaders are 'born and not made'. One leading writer in this field, Manfred Kets de Vries (1993), has rather aptly, commented that

> *When we plunge into the organisational literature on leadership, we quickly become lost in a labyrinth: there are endless definitions, countless articles and never-ending polemics. As far as leadership studies go, it seems that more and more has been studied about less and less, to end up ironically with a group of researchers who studied everything about nothing. It prompted one wit to say*

recently that reading the current world literature on leadership is rather like going through the Parisian telephone directory while trying to read it in Chinese!

2.1   Why is there a Growing Interest in Leadership?

Given the difficulty in pinning down the concept it is worth asking the question 'why the interest?' What is clear is that there are real business drivers, which seem to be:

- *The talent wars.* Evidence is emerging that organisations perceive the key to sustainable competitive advantage as being intricately involved with the ability to attract and retain a critical mass of talent in a world in which there is a shortage of the required talent.
- *A notable shift in the factors which drive investor decisions.* During the 1960s to the early 1990s, investor behaviour was dominated by 'hard' earnings data. However, since 1990 other 'intangible' factors have influenced this behaviour. In terms of these intangibles, investor views on the leadership of the organisation play a significant role.
- *To compete in a rapidly changing environment, the ability to lead and manage change is a critical success factor.* Yet authors, such as John Kotter (1990) from Harvard Business School, have estimated that some 70 % of change initiatives fail.
- *The changing nature of employee expectations.* People now come to work with new and different expectations. They increasingly expect to engage in meaningful and purposeful work and to have a say in how they operate. At the same time we have recognised that trust is an important factor in the way in which employees interact with their organisations and leaders. Many of these changes have resulted in a recognition that we need to engage employees with their organisations and their work in order to be able to enhance both individual and organisational performance.
- *Increasing levels of complexity.* In our attempts to manage and run organisations we have traditionally relied on developing systems and processes that attempt to enable us to operate the organisation as a

'well-oiled machine'. The mental model that underpins this aspiration, and related policies and practices, is one of organisation as a machine. Yet we now realise that all businesses operate in a complex environment and are, in reality, complex adaptive systems. This realisation underlies a recognition that operating in this context requires a different view of leadership; one that builds employee engagement and commitment and encourages agile and resilient practices.

- *New imperatives in terms of competition.* Increasingly responses to competitive threats and pressures require a new response. In order to develop and sustain a competitive advantage, organisations need to be increasingly creative and innovative. Furthermore, there is a growing need to develop creative thinking and innovative behaviour throughout the organisation by encouraging and rewarding these behaviours

- *Globalisation.* The world is becoming (some argue already is) a global village. Globalisation not only impacts markets, competitors and production costs, but increasingly leads to a shift in sources of skill and talent. For example, in the West there are insufficient new engineers graduating to cover the losses through retirement. However, in China and India a huge number of engineering graduates are created each year. In order to compete in a global talent market organisations need to determine new ways of acquiring and deploying their talent. Furthermore, organisations need to be able to understand the impact of significant cultural diversity in order to compete effectively in a global context.

Taken together the points above provide an imperative to reconsider the role of leadership and ranges of leadership competencies, practices and behaviours in order to enable future growth and survival.

2.2   Leadership or Management?

Before exploring the developments in our understanding of the nature of leadership it is useful to explore the debate around the differences between leadership and management. The historic inability to 'pin down' what is meant by leadership has led to a focus on developing effective management within organisations. During the 1960s, 1970s and early 1980s, organisations focused on building managerial competence as a means of securing competitive advantage. This resulted from the inability to *explain* and *predict* and thus be able to develop leadership. The managerial paradigm was much more suited to a rational approach to explanation, analysis and subsequent development than the more subjective and emotional concept of leadership. In the late 1990s, the resurging interest in leadership led to a perceived need to define the differences between leadership and management. While there are numerous and elaborate attempts to establish the differences, Peter Senge (1997) captured the essence of the difference in the statement that:

Managers do things right. Leaders do the right things.(p. 54)

This simple, but powerful, statement suggests that managers are focused on conformity, compliance, direction and control. On the other hand leaders are focused on possibilities, uncertainties, opportunities, vision and facilitating the contribution of others to build a successful business. In thinking about leadership and EI it may be helpful to review the differences between leadership and management summarised in Table 6.1.

Such a distinction invites the viewpoint that leadership is dynamic, positive and good, while management is negative, constraining and bureaucratic. In exploring the need for and nature of leadership in organisations the focus has been on seeking an alternative to the somewhat

Table 6.1 Differences between leadership and management

Leadership	Management
• Developing the vision of the future business	• Implementation and application
• Describing the path to achieve the vision	• Efficient and effective deployment of resources within business units
• Communicating the vision and path to all employees	
• Motivating employees to achieve the long-term goals	• Controlling
• Managing organisational change and transformation	• Monitoring and reviewing performance

negative managerial paradigm. This viewpoint is exaggerated when the media present leadership in the context of exciting and attractive entre-preneurial figures such as Richard Branson of Virgin.

However, in reality, it is evident that a truly successful organisation requires a combination of inspirational leadership with managerial effec-tiveness. If leaders are the organisation visionaries, then their relation-ship to managers may best be summed up by the established saying that: 'Vision without action is a dream. Action without vision is a nightmare.'

In the second decade of the twenty-first century we should recognise that a successful organisation needs both leadership and management. However, it may be that both dimensions need to be incorporated within individuals in influential or leading positions. Thus, leadership needs to be seen more as a set of behaviours and overall style of working than position within the organisation. Perhaps effective leadership needs to be viewed as combining vision and action. The concept of the leader/man-ager is perhaps what we need to be looking at as we move further into the new millennium.

2.3   The 'Long Line'

Although the level of interest in the idea of leadership and understand-ing what makes for effective leadership is at an all-time-high researchers, writers and observers have, for a long time, noted that top level leaders do make a difference. The academic research in this field has evolved based on the failures of previous frameworks to provide a clear explana-tion of what it takes to be a great leader. It is useful to reflect on how our thinking about the nature of effective leadership has developed over time (Higgs, 2003).

2.3.1   Trait Theory

The earliest structured and academic attempts to identify what makes for effective leadership were found in the early 1930s. This period was identi-fied with the concept of 'Trait Theory'. The focus was on examining the traits and characteristics associated with 'Great Men'. Interestingly, in this context leadership was perceived as a predominantly male characteristic or attribute. This approach to trying to understand leadership was based on attempting to tie down the common personality traits or characteristics associated with a range of figures (in both commerce and politics) that were widely perceived as 'great leaders'. However, the results of this approach were somewhat confusing and often contradictory. No clear overall or consistent pattern emerged and the conclusion was drawn that leadership could not be understood or predicted and leaders emerged, rather than resulted, from a clear pattern of behaviours or development. However, in exploring personality specifically, there are some enduring findings that remain relevant today. A number of studies, of all published research into personality and leadership found in reviews since the late 1950s until the late 1990s, have consistently found the following personality elements to predict leader effectiveness:

- conscientiousness,
- achievement drive, and
- cognitive abilities (IQ).

2.3.2   Behavioural/Style Theories

The failure of this 'Great Man' approach to offer a clear template for organisations coincided with a general focus on behaviourist thinking within organisations. This led to a second phase of leadership thinking and research, which may be broadly labelled as being a 'behavioural/style' approach. In essence, this was based on the premise that leadership was related to the behaviour and interpersonal style of leaders. The research and writing in this period (dominant in the 1960s) focused on linking humanistic models of work and organisational behaviour to leadership. Once again, the results of the research and reported studies were somewhat inconclusive and often contradictory.

2.3.3   Contingency Theories

The continuing interest in attempting to understand the behaviours or characteristics associated with effective leadership led to a focus on exploring the context within which leadership is exercised. During the

1970s this change of focus led to leadership being seen as being situationally or contextually determined. Within this framework, the nature of effective leadership was seen as being related to the leader's ability to adapt their behaviours to the needs of specific individuals or the context within which they were operating.

2.3.4 Transformational Leadership

In developing thinking about leadership many authors have proposed the importance of identifying what constitutes charismatic, inspirational and visionary leaders. Indeed, as stated earlier, these concepts go back as far as the early 1930s.However, over the past 25 years there has been a growing focus on these elements of leadership resulting in, what has been called, 'New Genre' leadership. This resulted in a need to shift the focus of leadership research and thinking from predominantly examining transactional models that were based on how leaders and followers exchanged with each other to models that might augment transactional leadership and were labelled charismatic, inspirational, transformational and visionary. Bass (1990), an influential writer on leadership within this 'New Genre', outlined a model that distinguished between transactional and transformational leadership. This distinction addresses, to an extent, both the leadership versus manager contribution and the role of leadership in an organisation. In addition, he highlights the relevance of distinction to the change context (something that we explored in Chapter 3). In broad terms Bass's model proposed that leadership is

> *a transformational influence process, often involving a restructuring of the situation and the perceptions of the members of the organisation.*(p. 125)

This statement may be understood in terms of:

> *Transformational leaders do the right things Transactional leaders do things right.*

Transformational leadership is about looking forward and being expansive, while transactional leadership is about the 'here and now' and about focusing on control.

Bass (1990) then proposed that transformational leadership is concerned with:

- *Charismatic behaviours*: Providing highly esteemed role models whom followers strive to emulate and who align others around a common vision, purpose and sense of direction.
- *Inspirational motivation*: Motivates and inspires others by providing meaning about the mission and its attainability.
- *Intellectual stimulation*: Encouraging followers to question basic conceptions and to consider problems from new and unique perspectives. Also encouraging others to be creative and innovative.
- *Individual consideration*: Paying special attention to each individual's needs for growth and personal achievement. Helping individuals to realise their potential and contribution through coaching and mentoring.

These elements of transformational leadership appear to be concerned with the relationships between the leaders and followers. In addition they seem to be focused on moving people towards the goals that the leader deems to be important. To achieve this movement (based on the construction of effective leader–follower relationships) would appear to call for: influence, intuitiveness, self-awareness, interpersonal sensitivity and motivation—all aspects of EI.

This model appears, particularly in relation to the transformational components, to address the leadership requirement for transformational change. However, much of the research into the validity of the model has focused on senior leader behaviours and, like much of the leadership research in the 1990s, has been dominated by the USA.

More recent UK research, conducted by Beverly Alimo-Metcalfe (1995) has attempted to capture followers' perceptions of leadership and to explore the leadership behaviour of both those at the top of the organisation (*distant* leaders) and those exercising dispersed leadership (*nearby* leaders). Based on this substantial UK research she has identified nine transformational leadership factors:

1. *Individualised consideration.* Largely along the lines of the factor proposed by Bass.

2. *Decisive, determined and achieving.* Leaders who make decisions, follow them through and achieve results.
3. *Involves others in discussion and formulation of vision, values and objectives.* Discusses not only the 'what', but also the 'how' and the relationship between the two.
4. *Networks actively.* Promotes the organisation/team and works closely with a range of stakeholders.
5. *Empowers individuals* and teams to act in line with agreed vision, values and objectives.
6. *Actively manages changes with sensitivity.* Is aware of the implications for, and impact of the changes, on others involved.
7. *Is genuinely accessible to followers.* Makes time available for others and is approachable.
8. *Is intellectually versatile.* Able to operate at a number of different levels ranging from big picture conceptualisation to detailed implementation and action.
9. *Is highly self-aware and acts with integrity.* Is open to input from others and change and able to be honest with himself/herself and others.

2.4   Leader Centricity

The above views of the nature of leadership are focused purely on the interaction between individuals rather than considering the requirements of the business or organisation. Thus leadership has been seen, in essence, as being a higher-order set of *enduring* personal skills or characteristics rather than as a means of achieving important longer-term organisational goals. During this somewhat lengthy period, the focus of attention was on the characteristics of the individual who was the designated leader. This tended, largely, to ignore the needs, interests and behaviours of these who 'were being led'. Within the above models the interaction between leaders and their followers was substantially examined as a one-way process rather than an interactive or iterative one. Over the course of many decades, the association of leadership with organisational success has become prevalent. This is due to the apparent links between the outstanding performance of a number of companies with a high profile Chief Executive (e.g., Bill Gates at Microsoft, Steve Jobs at Apple, Richard Branson at Virgin, Anita Roddick at Body Shop, Jack Welsh at General Electric).

This obsession with top leadership qualities has led to a refocusing of leadership research on 'top leaders'. The public profile of organisational leaders has always been higher in the USA than in the rest of the world. As a result, more recent leadership research has been focused on US corporations, and the top leadership teams. This focus has produced even more emphasis on personal qualities and on charismatic aspects of leadership. However, such bias is not without merit as it has provided some valuable insights into the behavioural aspects of outstanding leadership (in terms of producing significant organisational performance or transformation).

However, an exclusive focus on the top leaders can also be misleading. Many of the 'star' CEOs in the USA have, subsequently, been seen as flawed characters. For example, both Kenneth Ley of Enron and Bernie Webbers of Worldcom moved rapidly from role models to 'rogues' in 2002 amid allegations of fraud and business irregularities.

In exploring these issues Higgs (2009) found that these leaders were behaving in a way that focused on meeting their own goals and needs rather than serving the purpose of the organisation. He concluded that there is a need for understanding further the 'dark-side' leadership phenomenon and that the extant leadership literature does not really focus on this facet of leadership. Indeed, it has been pointed out frequently that the main focus of leadership studies and research has related to 'good' or effective leadership. In this context it has been noted, that few studies examine or explore leadership competences of flawed leadership. However, more recent events, such as the collapse of organisations such as Enron, Tyco, Worldcom and Lehman Brothers have prompted discussion and consideration of 'bad' leadership and reinforced calls for more empirical research to explore the nature, consequences and potential antecedents of 'bad' leadership.

Until relatively recently, the main focus of leadership research and writing has been dominated by a perception of leadership as associated with a position and by a focus on the extrinsic outcomes of either the characteristics or behaviours of the leader. Beverley Alimo-Metcalfe offered a critique of such an approach to exploring leadership. She suggested that decades of research in this vein provided little more than a discourse relating to the behaviour of white, male, American CEOs. Such a *'heroic' theory* of leadership has resulted in a plethora of definitions, contradictory research findings and general confusion. However, in spite of the evident limitations of this restricted view of leadership, the 'heroic' model continues to be influential. In January 2007, commenting on a special edition of the Harvard Business Review devoted to leadership, the journalist, Simon Caulkin (2007, p. 28) writing in *The Observer* commented that we continue to tend to see and position leaders as 'managers on steroids' and leadership as an occupation for 'lone he-men'. In essence, this 'heroic' view of leadership suggests a very leader-centric and limited view of the phenomenon. This can in itself be one of the reasons for our failure to 'discover the "Holy Grail" of leadership'. However, the tendency of such a theory of leadership to lead to organisational personality cults and follower dependence (resulting in lack of sustained performance) has not precluded continuing research activity and practitioner focus on the phenomenon viewed in this way. Indeed, there appears to be a core assumption that it is: *the leader who delivers organisational performance.*

Whilst there are a large number of definitions of leadership, a number of authors suggest an emerging core definitional framework that places more emphasis on the reciprocal relationship between leaders and followers. This comprises: (i) leadership being a social influence process; (ii) leadership being focused on the achievement of specific goals; and (iii) leadership being concerned with both means and ends. It is perhaps this framing of the construct that captures the move from a direct linkage between the leader's behaviours and organisational outcomes to a more indirect linkage in which the followers' behaviours or capabilities mediate the relationship. Some research sees this as a process of leaders' behaviours creating a climate that enables effective performance by followers.

Other views and research are captured within the transformational model described above. There is little doubt that this latter view has dominated leadership studies over the past 10–15 years. An important aspect of the transformational leadership model (that has become dominant in thinking about the topic) is that of the leader as being a visionary. It is perhaps this component of the transformational framework that continues the 'heroic' link encountered in many previous models. The framework continues to emphasise leader-centric behaviours. It is evident that leader centricity results in follower dependence that limits the scope for creativity and innovation. Furthermore it increases the potential for 'bad' leadership to emerge. However, while there are, in the literature, numerous descriptions of 'bad' leadership behaviours there do appear to be a number of central (albeit overlapping) themes that occur when considering 'bad' or 'dark-side' leadership:

1. *Abuse of power.* This encompasses the abuse of power to serve personal goals or achieve personal gain; the use of power to reinforce self-image and enhance perceptions of personal performance; and the abuse of power to conceal personal inadequacies.
2. *Inflicting damage on others.* This focuses on negative impact on subordinates and includes: bullying; coercion; negative impact on perceptions of subordinate self-efficacy; damage to the psychological well-being of subordinates; and inconsistent or arbitrary treatment of subordinates.
3. *Over-exercise of control to satisfy personal needs.* Obsession with detail/ perfectionism and limiting subordinate initiative.
4. *Rule breaking to serve own purposes.* This is the area of behaviour in which leaders engage in corrupt, unethical and, indeed, illegal behaviours. The ability of leaders to engage in 'bad' behaviour is seen to arise from their positional power.

In terms of the relatively limited empirical research into 'bad' leadership, there has been some evidence that it leads to dysfunctional performance within the organisation. Whilst some argue that 'bad' leadership can result in short-term performance success, others point out that it will inevitably lead to long-term problems and dysfunctional performance. What is notable, however, is that the 'bad' leadership studies (unlike the conventional leadership studies) are more focused on the internal effects of leader behaviours than the external performance outcomes. Studies have shown, for example, consistent adverse effects on followers, subjected to 'bad' leadership, in terms of job satisfaction, affective commitment and psychological well-being. Each of these areas is shown in the broader organisational behaviour literature to be related to longer-term organisational performance. Thus, the impact of 'bad' leadership tends to be felt in the longer term through the debilitating impact on morale and motivation of subordinates.

3   Recent Developments in Leadership Thinking

The diverse, and often contradictory, findings on the nature of effective leadership, outlined above, appear to share two common factors: (i) focus on top-level leaders, and (ii) the measure of success employed is the financial performance of the business. This criticism implies an alternative means of assessing the effectiveness of leadership behaviours, in terms of the impact of leader behaviours on the followers. In addition, it has been suggested that the extensive literature on leadership, and changing schools of thought and models, contains much reworking of earlier concepts. Perhaps the frustration with the inability of leadership research is rooted in a paradigm, which suggests that there is a fundamental truth, which is yet to be discovered. If the view of sensemaking proposed by Karl Weick (1995) is considered, a new way forward may be found. He proposed that:

> *Social and organisational sciences, as opposed to physics or biology, do not discover anything new, but let us comprehend what we have known all along in a much better way, opening up new, unforeseen, possibilities of reshaping, re-engineering and restructuring our original social environment.* (p. 76)

Shifting the lens through which leadership is observed, in line with the above thought, may bring new and useful insights. Perhaps an alternative lens has already been identified, although not made explicit. A number of authors have asserted that the influence of Weberian rationality on organisations has begun to wane, and this decline is accompanied by a recognition of emotional realities. Viewing leadership through this lens suggests a potential change in the measure of leadership effectiveness from hard business results to the impact of leaders on their followers and, in turn, on the organisational climate. This view resonates with the view that leadership, in a context that is marked by volatility, uncertainty, complexity and ambiguity, requires focus on building the capability of people within the organisation to deal with these new contexts.

Illustrative of these more recent models of leadership thinking are:

- *Authentic leadership*: a pattern of transparent and ethical leader behaviour that encourages openness in sharing information needed to make decisions while accepting followers' inputs.
- *Ethical leadership*: the demonstration of normatively appropriate conduct through personal actions and interpersonal relationships, and the promotion of such conduct to followers.
- *Cognitive leadership*: a broad range of approaches to leadership emphasising how leaders and followers think and process information.
- *Complexity leadership*: Many previous models of leadership have been designed to accommodate more traditional hierarchical structures of organisations. To the degree that organisations are hierarchical, so too are leadership models. Yet, there has been a growing sense of tension in the leadership literature that models of leadership that were designed for the past century may not fully capture the leadership dynamic of organisations operating in today's knowledge-driven economy. According to complex-systems leadership theory, leadership can be enacted through *any interaction* in an organisation. Thus, leadership is an *emerging* phenomenon within complex systems and can be seen as widely distributed.
- *Shared leadership*: Shared (or team) leadership capacity is an emergent state; something dynamic that develops throughout a team's lifespan and that varies based on the inputs, processes and outcomes of the team. It produces patterns of reciprocal influence, which reinforce and develop further relationships between team members
- *Leader Member Exchange (LMX)*: The central principle in LMX theory is that leaders develop different exchange relationships with their followers, whereby the quality of the relationship alters the impact on important leader and member outcomes. Thus, leadership occurs when leaders and followers are able to develop effective relationships that result in mutual and incremental influence.

3.1   The Leader and the Organisation

The developments outlined above all tend to point to a need to consider leadership in the context of the organisation. Indeed, in presenting her research on leadership, Beverly Alimo-Metcalfe highlights that the organisational context and situational considerations relating to leadership were not adequately considered in many of the earlier leadership theories. In terms of the leadership setting it is important to balance the organisation's strategy and vision, culture and people with the leadership requirement. This is not purely an analysis of individual components in a state of stasis; rather it is a question of considering how the dynamic equilibrium between these three dimensions is maintained. To a large extent, the maintenance of the dynamic equilibrium may be seen as occurring through a process of organisational learning and adjustment.

While the leadership context is clearly dynamic the requirement of effective leadership is also *dynamic*. This dynamic requires a balance between the personality or make-up of the leader, the leader's behaviour and the leader's overall cognitive models or 'mind maps'. An effective leader uses constant feedback from many sources and adapts each component through a process of individual learning. This dynamic is summarised in Fig. 6.1.

Much of the research and writing on leadership and organisation focuses on one or other of the models outlined in Figs. 6.1 and 6.2.

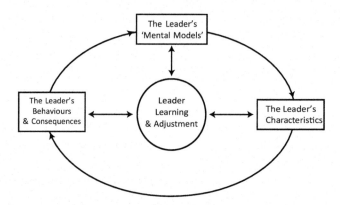

Fig. 6.1 The leadership requirement

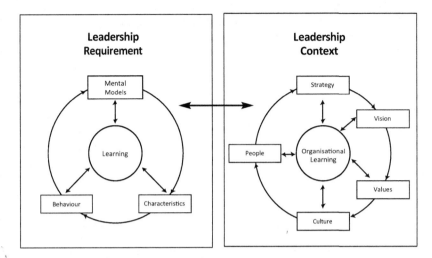

Fig. 6.2   The dynamics of leadership

However, in reality there is a relationship between the two. At the simplest level we can understand that how a leader conceptualises their business world impacts the formulation of strategy. However, the very conceptualisation of the strategy is, eventually, impacted by the reality of the organisational learning resulting from its attempted implementation. Thus, leaders' impact on the organisations and, in a dynamic sense, the reality of the organisational experience impacts on the leaders. This is the relationship summarised in Fig. 6.2.

Leadership is therefore about managing the dynamics between these two viewpoints and ensuring the effective performance of both individuals and the organisation. Within this dynamic model there is an important shift to considering leader behaviours and the ability of leaders to build the capability of their followers to adapt to change and deliver the strategic goals. Although not explicitly acknowledging this shift in view on the nature of leadership, there is a body of literature, which is beginning to look at leadership through a 'new lens' to attempt to make sense of a complex, concept in today's business environment.

This 'emerging school' encompasses elements of other approaches already described. Within this 'emerging theory' school of thought there are two common strands:

- the focus of study is on what leaders actually do; and
- the determinant of effectiveness includes the leader's impact on followers and their subsequent ability to perform.

It may have been Kotter's (1995) study that prompted a move from studying personality, or testing theoretical models in the search for understanding of the nature of leadership. His study of the work of leaders is certainly seen to influence many of the studies that may be placed in this 'emerging school'. Typical of these studies is the work reported by Kouzes and Posner (1998) that identified the following elements of effective leadership (with effectiveness judged from the follower's perspective):

- *Challenging the process.* A constant questioning of why things are being done in a certain way combined with openness to having their own actions challenged.
- *Inspiring shared vision.* Engaging others with a vision of how things can be and how progress may be made.
- *Enabling others to act.* Working on a belief in the potential of people and creating the conditions to enable people to realise their potential.
- *Modelling the way.* Acting as a role model and demonstrating integrity in terms of congruence of words and actions.
- *Encouraging the heart.* Providing recognition tailored to an understanding of the needs and personalities of each person.

When reviewing these findings clear overlaps with elements of transformational leadership and the more recent models (see above) become apparent. However, this does not diminish the potential contribution of Kouzes and Posner when seen in a 'sensemaking' context. A further illustration of the 'emerging school' is provided by the research of Goffee and Jones (2000) who identify the following behaviours of effective leaders:

- *Approachability and vulnerability.* Willingness to expose personal weaknesses, thus revealing their humanity and approachability.

- *Intuitive in dealing with 'soft' data.* Using 'soft' data to judge the nature and timing of interventions.
- *Tough empathy.* Empathising genuinely, but realistically and caring about what people do.
- *Reveal differences.* Capitalise on what is unique about them.

Goffee and Jones are quite explicit in their acknowledgement that a number of 'effective' leaders they studied would not, necessarily, have been considered so in the absence of the follower's perspective.

When reviewing studies such as those outlined above, it becomes evident that this 'emerging school' sees leadership as being a combination of personal characteristics and areas of competence. This relatively simple statement has significant implications for the way in which we view leadership. The personality of the leader plays a part in the exercise of leadership. The areas of effectiveness (the 'skills') need to be exercised in a way that is congruent with the underlying personality of the leader. Building on this view it is possible to suggest a model that reflects the research and thinking on leadership emerging from a 'sensemaking' paradigm. This model is shown in Fig. 6.3.

The elements in this model are explored briefly below:

(a) Skill/Competence Areas

- *Envision*—the ability to identify a clear future picture that will inform the way in which people direct their efforts and utilise their skills.
- *Engage*—finding the appropriate way for each individual to understand the vision and, hence, the way in which they can contribute.
- *Enable*—acting on a belief in the talent and potential of individuals, and creating the environment in which these can be realised.
- *Inquire*—being open to real dialogue with those involved in the organisation and encouraging free and frank debate of all issues.
- *Develop*—working with people to build their capability and help them to make the envisioned contribution.

• Envision • Engage • Enable • Inquire • Develop	Skills/Competencies
• Authenticity • Integrity • Will • Self-Belief • Self-Awareness	Being Yourself

Fig. 6.3   An emerging model of effective leadership

(b) Personal Characteristics

- *Authenticity*—being genuine and not attempting to 'play a role', not acting in a manipulative way.
- *Integrity*—acting with integrity; being consistent in what you say and do.
- *Will*—a drive to lead, and persistence in working towards a goal.
- *Self-belief*—a realistic evaluation of your capabilities and belief that you can achieve required goals.
- *Self-awareness*—a realistic understanding of 'who you are', how you feel and how others see you.

In addition to the above we do need to remember that cognitive abilities (IQ) also contribute to leader effectiveness.

4   Emotional Intelligence and Leadership

Over the past few years many have claimed that effective leadership requires high levels of EI. For example, Daniel Goleman (Goleman, Boyatzis & McKee, 2002), a leading proponent of EI, claims that while EI is more important than IQ and technical skill, the level of importance is even greater for leadership roles. Indeed, in one radio interview he claimed that the higher one progresses in an organisation, the more important EI becomes. Such views have been supported by prominent academics in the leadership arena (e.g., Professors Warren Bennis, Roger Gill) and senior businessmen (e.g., Tim Melville-Ross—former Director General of the Institute of Directors and Sir John Egan—former CEO of Jaguar Cars and BAA).

These claims can be seen as feasible in the light of how we have seen leadership thinking and research developing. From the above discussion it is evident that, although we cannot produce a concise definition of leadership we can identify a number of important components. Thus, leadership in today's organisation may be seen to require:

- focusing on the needs of individuals;
- decisiveness;
- achievement;
- involving and engaging others in formulating vision and values;
- integrating the internal and external stakeholders;
- empowering followers;
- managing change;
- being accessible, available and open;
- intellectual versatility;
- self-awareness;
- open to feedback and adaptable;
- able to learn; and
- working with integrity.

The elements of leadership for today's context, outlined in the preceding section, either imply, or directly state, that leadership requires the following elements of EI:

- interpersonal sensitivity,
- emotional resilience,
- self-awareness,
- influence,
- conscientiousness,
- intuitiveness, and
- motivation.

If these are the requirements of effective leadership then EI clearly provides an indication of leadership potential. This potential relationship is summarised in Table 6.2.

In addition to the 'mapping' of the components of EI onto the emergent leadership components outlined above, both Table 6.1 and Figure 6.1 point to the need for 'balance'. The concept of 'balance' with EI has already been explored in Chapter 3. The view of leadership outlined in this chapter emphasises the importance of achieving this balance. The emerging view of the requirements for effective leadership and the evidence on the nature of EI does, to an extent, overlap. Chapter 3 has provided some insights into the nature of this relationship.

In order to explore the suggestion that EI might be related more broadly to leadership, Malcolm Higgs and Deborah Rowland (2000) conducted a content analysis of the transformational-leadership models and the work of authors classified above as being in the emerging theory area. Using this analysis and a review of the various models above we have mapped EI elements onto a range of leadership models. This analysis is shown in Table 6.3. From this, it is evident that there is a theoretical case for a broader link between EI and leadership.

Table 6.2 Emotional intelligence and leadership

Elements of EI	Elements of effective leadership
• Self-awareness	• Focus on needs of others
• Conscientiousness	• Decisiveness
• Motivation	• Achievement
• Emotional resilience	• Involvement
• Intuitiveness	• Integrating stakeholders
• Influence	• Empower others
• Interpersonal sensitivity	• Manage change
	• Accessible and open
	• Intellectually versatile
	• Self-awareness
	• Open to feedback
	• Able to learn
	• Integrity

4.1 Evidence of Relationships Between Emotional Intelligence and Leadership

Whilst Table 6.3 outlines the conceptual linkages between EI and leadership it is important to demonstrate that these apply in practice. A number of studies have found such relationships employing a number of different models of EI (see Chapter 5 for details of the different models). Using our own model (outlined above) a range of empirical studies have demonstrated strong relationships between EI and aspects of leadership.

4.1.1 Emotional Intelligence and Leadership Levels

Based on a sample of 100 senior managers and directors we found statistically significant differences in overall levels of EI and level in organisations. It was found that CEOs had higher levels of EI than other directors who, in turn, had higher EI levels than senior managers. Whilst EI clearly made a difference we found no statistically significant differences in terms of the IQ of participants. Interestingly this showed a similar relationship to Goleman's report of the impact of EI on the success of graduates in rising through an organisational hierarchy in their careers.

4.1.2 Emotional Intelligence and Leadership Potential

A study was conducted that explored the relationship between EI and an overall rating of potential to move into senior level positions within the public sector in New Zealand. Some 90 participants were tracked through eight structured assessment centres. Prior to attending the centre all participants completed an EI questionnaire. The results from these questionnaires were compared to the assessors' combined ratings of top leadership potential. Strong relationships exist between the overall EI scores of participants and ratings of their potential. In addition, all elements of EI, with the exception of 'intuitiveness', were found to be

Table 6.3 Relationships between leadership 'models' and emotional intelligence

Elements of EI	Leadership models								
	Trait	Behaviour/style	Transformational (Bass)	Transformational (Alimo-Metcalfe)	Authentic	Ethical	LMX	Shared	Complexity
Self-awareness				o			o	o	
Emotional resilience					o		o	o	o
Motivation	o	o	o	o	o		o	o	
Interpersonal sensitivity		o	o	o	o	o	o	o	o
Influence		o	o	o	o		o	o	
Intuitiveness			o	o	o				o
Conscientiousness	o		o	o	o	o			

related to the potential ratings. In this study we also found that IQ was a contributing factor to ratings of potential, as were a number of broad managerial competencies.

4.1.3 Emotional Intelligence and Leader Performance and Follower Commitment

In a large-scale study of officers and ratings in the UK Royal Navy (around 250) a questionnaire was completed by participants that included scales looking at EI together with measures of perceived leadership effectiveness and follower commitment. The results showed that EI was significantly related to both of these dimensions. In addition the results were further validated using separate measures of actual performance.

4.1.4 Emotional Intelligence and Change Leadership

In the following chapter we will be exploring the topic of change leadership in some detail. However, in an earlier study the relationships between EI and change-leadership competencies were explored. Using a sample of 74 managers, the results of the study showed strong relationships between the change-leadership competencies and all but one ('intuitiveness') of the elements of EI.

Although the evidence from these (and other) studies shows a clear relationship between EI and the emerging models of leadership for today's context, more research is required to explore the relationship between EI and other factors (e.g., IQ, managerial competencies) in explaining leadership effectiveness. However, while more research is clearly needed we are prompted to speculate that effective leadership may well be a combination of EI, IQ and managerial competence. In a similar way to our earlier work we might see the formula for leadership effectiveness (LQ) as being:

$$EQ + IQ + MQ = LQ$$

What is also clear, from the information available is that different organisations in differing business contexts need different types of leaders. However, when we look at the elements that comprise EI, we see that different elements assume differing significance in changing situations in which leaders face differing contexts in which they operate. However, before making too many claims, we need to remember that EI is a complex concept that encompasses seven elements. As mentioned, differing situations may require differing balances of these elements to provide effective leadership. For example, in national leadership, the required profile in a national crisis (such as a war, or economic crisis) may be significantly different to that in a time of peace and prosperity. To illustrate this in a UK context, during World War II the leader of the UK needed to be extremely high on:

- emotional resilience,
- influence,
- intuitiveness, and
- motivation.

There can be little doubt that Winston Churchill exhibited all these elements. However, it is important to bear in mind that these elements are not only required in a crisis. They are *enduring* elements that assume different significance in crisis situations.

In the totally different context of the early 2000s with the UK enjoying a period of relative economic affluence and stability, but recovering from a bruising transformation of business life and exposure to business and governmental 'scandals', the elements of EI at a premium for political leaders were:

- self-awareness,
- conscientiousness,
- interpersonal sensitivity,
- motivation (new goals), and
- emotional resilience (adhering to economic disciplines).

Again, there is little doubt that then Prime Minister Tony Blair appeared to exhibit a number of these elements of EI.

While we can dispute these national (and UK-biased) examples we can all think of more concrete examples related to the leadership of our own organisations. However, whether operating at the national (and theoretical) level or more specific (and practical) level we can also recognise specific situations in which the dominant requirements are offset by the lesser requirements. Although there will be differing priorities on the elements of EI, in all cases a *balance* is needed. For example, Winston Churchill may have faced situations as a leader in which he needed to display interpersonal sensitivity within an overall context that did not place a premium on this. Similarly, Tony Blair faced situations in which he needed to display intuitiveness even though not a priority in the overall context.

What we do seem to know about EI is that, given an average level of IQ it predicts success in terms of advancement in an organisation. Thus, it would seem that emotionally intelligent leaders should be able to lead organisations through periods of significant or transformational change. While the evidence for this relationship is only just beginning to emerge in academic terms, what we do know from experience is that organisations that have been successful in achieving significant transformation have leaders who exhibit different qualities from those associated with successful *management* of stable organisations. Furthermore, such leaders have been successful in transforming the behaviours of large numbers of key players within their organisations. Thus, leadership in these situations is a 'team' rather than a 'solo' game. The top individual leaders have not only demonstrated significant personal levels of EI but also encouraged or released the EI of other leaders within their organisations.

5   Summary and Conclusion

In this chapter we have explored the increasing importance of effective leadership within organisations facing a volatile, uncertain, complex and ambiguous environment. We have hopefully shown the way in which our thinking about, and models of, leadership have evolved to reflect changing needs and contexts.

It is clear that earlier statements about the importance of EI for effective leadership are more than rhetoric—they are grounded in empirical evidence. However, EI is evidently not a 'silver bullet' that explains all that we need to know about leadership. From the ideas about, and research into, leadership that we have discussed, it is hopefully evident that we do need to see leadership as comprising a mixture of EI, cognitive competencies and broader managerial competencies. It is this combination that underpins the idea of leading with EI. Indeed we will return to this, and develop it further in Chapter 8.

The importance of the dynamic between the leadership requirement and the leadership context has been highlighted in this chapter. In the next chapter we will explore the context within which leadership is exercised with a particular focus on the context of increasing needs for organisations to implement significant changes. In doing this we will consider how change leadership draws on the theories and models that we have examined and how leadership behaviours and practices can contribute to change success.

Bibliography

Alimo-Metcalfe, B. (1995). An investigation of female and male constructs of leadership. *Women in Management Review, 10,* 3–8.

Bass, B. M. (1990). From transactional to transformational leadership: Learning to share the vision. *Organizational Dynamics, 18*(3), 19–31.

Caulkin, S. (2007). On leadership. *Observer,* January, p. 28.

Goffee, R., & Jones, G. (2000). Why should anyone be led by you? *Harvard Business Review,* September–October, 63–70.

Goleman, D., Boyatzis, R. E., & McKee, A. (2002). *Primal leadership: Realizing the power of emotional intelligence.* Boston, MA: Harvard Business School Press.

Higgs, M. J. (2003). Developments in leadership thinking. *Leadership and Organization Development Journal, 24,* 273–284.

Higgs, M. J. (2009). The good, the bad and the ugly: Leadership and narcissism. *Journal of Change Management, 9,* 165–178.

Higgs, M. J., & Rowland, D. (2000). Building change leadership capability: The quest for change competence. *Journal of Change Management, 1,* 116–130.

Kets de Vries, M. F. R. (1993). *Leaders, fools and imposters: Essays on the psychology of leadership.* San Francisco, CA: Jossey-Bass.

Kotter, J. P. (1990). *A force for change: How leadership differs from management.* New York: Simon & Schuster.

Kotter, J. P. (1995). Leading change: Why transformation efforts fail. *Harvard Business Review,* May–June, 11–16.

Kouzes, J. R., & Posner, B. F. (1998). *Encouraging the heart.* San Francisco, CA: Jossey-Bass.

Senge, P. M. (1997). Communities of leaders and learners. *Harvard Business Review, 75*(5), 30–31.

Weick, K. E. (1995). *Sensemaking in organisations.* Thousand Oaks, CA: Sage.

7

The Leadership Context

1 Introduction

In the previous chapter we explored developments in our thinking about the nature of leadership and the way in which we can develop leadership that will be effective in achieving key organisational goals. In doing this we alluded to the changing context in which leadership is enacted. In this chapter we explore in more detail the context facing organisations today and the related impact this has on leadership.

It is widely agreed that the context in which most organisations operate today is one of volatility, uncertainty, complexity and ambiguity. Our models of organisations are beginning to be recognised as needing to change. For many decades, the dominant way in which we saw organisations was through the metaphor of the organisation as a machine. This underpinned our approach to organising work and structuring the organisation. Within the manufacturing sector, we saw the dominance of practices of mass production that were dominated by the concepts associated with 'Taylorism' (and what has been referred to as 'Fordism'). This resulted in the pervasive use of the production line. This mind-set was taken up in the design and structuring of all types of work. We saw the

© The Editor(s) (if applicable) and the Author(s) 2016
M. Higgs, V. Dulewicz, *Leading with Emotional Intelligence*,
DOI 10.1007/978-3-319-32637-5_7

introduction of techniques such as work measurement into the realm of 'white collar' work. Within this view of organisations, there is an emphasis on control. However, over the past few decades the ability to engineer an organisation as a machine has created significant problems in relation to the ability to compete successfully and to adapt to changing circumstances.

Both organisations and researchers are now seeing that to succeed in the new context requires rethinking our organisational metaphor. Organisations are now increasingly being viewed through the metaphor of organisation as a living organism. There is a realisation that organisations are, in reality, complex adaptive systems. Given this view there is a move from a focus on control to one of facilitating the system to achieve required outcomes.

It is evident that these shifts in the context within which organisations operate have significant implications in terms of the role, practices and behaviours of leaders.

The major issues to consider in understanding the leadership context in more detail are:

- *Complexity*: The need to consider strategies that will work within an increasingly complex environment.
- *Employee commitment and engagement*: In moving away from a control dominated and 'engineering' mind-set to a facilitating one that requires employees to be fully engaged with, and committed to, their work and the organisation.
- *Change*: In a volatile, uncertain, complex and ambiguous context organisations face an increasing need to change and develop the capability to be agile and resilient.

Taken together these contextual shifts give rise to a need for leaders to be able to enable organisations to respond to and implement change effectively. Therefore, we do need to consider what is required of *effective change leaders*.

We will now consider each of these contextual factors in more detail.

1.1   Complexity

In considering organisations as complex adaptive systems it is inevitable that change will be a constant. Indeed it is evident that there is a growing realisation that change in itself is a complex process. More recent research into organisations and change, has considered the emerging field of complexity theory and the associated development of the 'new sciences' as a source of understanding of organisational behaviour and change. A number of authors recognise the difficulties of constructing structured approaches to the management of organisations and argue that using evolutionary theory may lead to greater insight into organisational realities and developments. In applying evolutionary theory to organisations, it is important to distinguish between complicated systems and complex systems. Complicated systems are rich in detail whereas complex systems are rich in structure. Reflecting on this distinction it can be argued that the root of many of the challenges and difficulties faced by organisations is that leaders are trained to solve complicated problems rather than complex ones. Thus, leaders view change, in particular, as a problem that can be analysed and then solved in a linear or sequential manner. However, complex problems require leaders to cope with dilemmas in the system rather than to arrive at definitive solutions.

In applying evolutionary theory to organisations and the changes that they face there are three models of evolution: natural selection, probability and complexity.

- *Natural selection*: The fittest or most adapted to the environment are selected; there is a gradual steady rate of change that is only visible over a long period of time; variation occurs by chance, not intent.
- *Probability*: Change results from historic contingency; change may be seen as punctuated equilibrium; sources of change are external
- *Complexity*: Organisations are self-organising; organisations are in a process of continual adaptation; change is influenced by sensitivity to initial conditions; change in non-linear; there are increasing returns from changes; change is notable for the emergence of novelty.

The natural selection and probability views of evolution are most closely associated with the 'traditional' approaches to the development and management of organisations and associated approaches to dealing with change. However, the complexity view of evolution appears to be the most relevant to today's context. If the organisation views its evolution in the light of the complexity view then transformations or developments are effected when the knowledge required for a new form is embodied in a community of practice and is operated by individuals, groups, structures, policies and programmes or networks. In line with this, Blackmore (1998) argues that evolution and change in organisations is a process of displacement where older, less well-adapted technologies or 'strategic memes' are replaced by newer forms.

From the above it is evident that the way in which we view organisations needs to move to a complexity view if they are to develop in the volatile, uncertain, complex and ambiguous environment in which they now operate. It is equally clear that this shift in mind-set and related practices have significant implications for leaders in today's organisations. Given the need to embed changes and developments in groups and individuals it can be argued that we need to build people's commitment to the developments and engage them with the organisation and the changes that are required in order to evolve and cope with complexity.

2   Employee Commitment and Engagement

There is an enormous growth in the interest in how employees engage with their organisations. In part, this results from the changes in the context in which organisations now operate. In today's environment, there has been a recognition that high levels of employee commitment and engagement (these terms tend to be used interchangeably) are important to the achievement of high levels of performance. Indicative of this is the extent to which organisations undertake annual employee engagement or commitment surveys and use this data to inform organisational and leadership behaviours, policies and practices.

In order to understand what is behind this belief in the importance of this development it is useful to explore the concept of employee commitment in more detail. Far from being a new concept, organisational commitment is one of the most enduring and widely researched concepts in the field of organisational behaviour and leadership. It has tended to characterise the relationship between an individual and an organisation since the 1980s, and along with the job satisfaction, organisational commitment has emerged as a powerful attitudinal predictor of performance outcomes. More recently the construct has been linked to that of employee engagement, and has even been seen as a component of engagement. Research into the link between organisational policies and practices (specifically those that impact employees) and organisational performance has shown that the leaders play an important, if neglected, role in this link and can have a strong impact on employee attitudes such as organisational commitment. Such findings are consistent with research from leadership literature (e.g., leader–member exchange and transformational leadership) that shows that the relationship between a leader and follower may be related to outcomes at the individual and organisational levels, including organisational commitment.

Although some studies have tested models of relationships between various antecedents of organisational commitment these have often focused on the impact of the leader. Whilst job characteristics such as task significance and personal characteristics (e.g., self-efficacy) have also been studied, to date there has been limited investigation of the relative impact of a range of different antecedents on organisational commitment.

Organisational commitment is, typically, seen as a multidimensional construct. An early and influential view was that organisational commitment is 'the relative strength of an individual's identification with and involvement in a particular organisation'. It is underpinned by three factors: a strong belief in and acceptance of the organisation's goal and values; a willingness to exert considerable effort on behalf of the organisation; and a strong desire to retain membership in the organisation. More recently, Allen and Meyer's (1990) three-component model has become the dominant conceptualisation of commitment. This proposes three types of commitment, which are different in terms of the nature of the relationship that maintains the individual's membership in the organisation. These are:

1. *Affective commitment*: the employees' emotional attachment to, identification with, and involvement in, the organisation;
2. *Normative commitment*: based on feelings of loyalty and obligation; and
3. *Continuance commitment*: the commitment based on the costs that employees associate with leaving the organisation.

Many studies of organisational commitment have focused on affective commitment—although the broader term organisational commitment is often employed. Affective commitment has been demonstrated to have a strong correlation with job satisfaction that, in turn, is related to performance. Affective commitment is seen as a specific reflection of an underlying overall job attitude and as a component of 'state engagement'.

In terms of affective commitment, its importance lies in its relationship to outcomes at both the individual and organisational levels. It has been linked to attendance, performance, organisational citizenship behaviour and, negatively, to absenteeism and turnover. Affective commitment has shown stronger correlations with outcomes than either normative or continuance commitment. A wide range of personal and situational factors have been identified as antecedents of affective commitment. Personal characteristics include age, gender, organisational tenure and education, person-organisation fit, and self-efficacy. Situational characteristics include job and organisational characteristics as well as work experiences. The most researched situational characteristics in terms of affective commitment are job characteristics and leadership (particularly in terms of involvement and participative decision-making). While leadership has been seen to have an impact on the broad construct of organisational commitment, there seems to have been inadequate research that has focussed specifically on the relationship of the leader and affective commitment. However, some research in this area has shown that perceptions of leadership behaviour have been demonstrated to be significantly related to organisational commitment, as well as to aspects of the job experience including job autonomy, sense of achievement and to job challenge as well as to outcomes including discretionary effort. Accordingly, leaders are critical for the implementation of policies and practices that impact employees' practices and their behaviours are critical for employee satisfaction with them and with outcomes at the individual and organisational levels. Improving the capabilities of leaders in people management is thus an important task for organisations.

In exploring the development of commitment and the leader's role it is worth noting that the literature on transformational leadership and on leader–member exchange provides additional support for the potential impact of leaders on organisational commitment. It is notable that these findings relate to leadership theories that are engaging and facilitating rather than overly leader centric. Within the broader view of leadership as a distributed function is increasing evidence that engaging leadership is positively associated with work attitudes and behaviours at an individual and organisational level. Such leaders transform enable their followers to realise their aspirations, encourage them to achieve their full potential and provide meaning and challenge, thereby enhancing follower's level of self-efficacy, confidence, meaning and self-determination and their greater sense of empowerment.

Whilst leader behaviours are a clear antecedent of affective commitment, in a recent study Higgs and McBain (2009) found that there were two further important factors, which had a positive impact on commitment. These were:

2.1   Nature of Work

It was noted above that perceptions of the leader are related to aspects of the job experience since the leader has a critical role in setting the context for performance. However, in this study the nature of work that has emerged is a very important facet of the job and an important situational influence on employee attitudes. The research suggested that the nature of the work employees undertake possesses intrinsically motivating characteristics, with five core dimensions: skill variety, task identity, task significance, autonomy and feedback. The inclusion of high levels of these characteristics produced higher levels of motivation, work performance, job satisfaction and organisational commitment.

2.2   Autonomy and Control

Within the literature on the nature of work autonomy has been identified as one of the core dimensions of jobs or work roles. In addition to such situational factors, the Higgs and McBain (2009) study indicated the importance of personal characteristics and the interaction of these with the work context as antecedents of organisational commitment. One finding that is relevant in this context is that of the importance of self-efficacy or a person's judgement of their capabilities to organise and execute courses of action required to attain designated types of performances. Self-efficacy was shown to be correlated with organisational commitment. It was also found that a sense of empowerment was an important component of autonomy. In particular, it was empowerment that enabled individual freedom to contribute to the way in which they performed their job roles that was important. The extent to which employees have belief in having the resources to carry out work tasks and roles successfully and the extent to which they are empowered to do so have implications for individual motivation and impact on commitment. Furthermore, it seems that it is the creation of conditions that lead to autonomous motivation that has the most significant impact on the development of positive organisational commitment. It appeared that autonomous motivation resulted from a combination of: the nature and design of the work itself; the behaviour of the leader in creating a climate that enhances the possibilities for an individual to realise a sense of autonomy; and related motivation that leads to a higher level of organisational commitment.

Reviewing the above summary of commitment and engagement, and its importance to organisations in today's context, it is evident that leaders need to adopt a more *involving and engaging style* and to focus on developing a climate that enables employees to contribute and perform effectively.

3   The Challenge of Change

According to many authors, up to 70 % of change initiatives fail (e.g., Higgs & Rowland, 2005; Kotter, 1995). However, there is a growing need for organisations to implement major changes in order to be able to respond in a business environment that is becoming increasingly volatile and complex. So what are the reasons for consistent failure and what leads to success?

The problem of failing to manage change is illustrated by Buchanan and Boddy (1992). They report the results of a survey that showed that mangers have neither the expertise, nor capacity, to implement change successfully and that managing change according to textbook theory is difficult. A further reason for the failure of change is argued to be that the prevailing theoretical paradigms are based on assumptions that: (1) managers can choose successful mutations in advance of environmental changes; (2) change is a linear process; and (3) organisations are systems tending to states of stable equilibrium. This paradigm has a long history, perhaps beginning with Lewin (1951) who proposed the classic three-stage model of the change process. These three stages are:

- *Unfreeze*: This stage is about creating the case for change and ensuring that there is dissatisfaction with the status quo.
- *Mobilise*: Mobilising focuses on identifying and mobilising the resources required to effect the change
- *Refreeze*: This phase focuses on embedding new ways of working in the organisation.

The centrality of this 'mental model' is illustrated by Kotter's (1995) study of the reasons for failure of major transformational initiatives. The key causes he identified were:

- *Allowing too much complacency*: Failing to create a compelling case for the change and allowing people to believe that the status quo is tenable.
- *Failing to develop a sufficiently powerful guiding coalition*: Not paying sufficient attention to building a coalition of key influencers and champions of the change.
- *Underestimating the power of vision*: Failing to develop a compelling and tangible vision of the desired future state.
- *Insufficient communication of the vision*: Over-reliance on initial communication of the vision and failing to embed the communication of

the vision in the day-to-day conversations that occur in the organisation.

* *Allowing obstacles to block the implementation of the vision*: Giving up the change implementation if significant obstacles to the change arise.
* *Failure to create short-term wins*: Transformational change takes place over an extended period. It is important to secure short-term results that indicate that the change is moving forward.
* *Declaring victory too soon*: Failure can arise if the change is declared to have succeeded before it has been fully implemented.
* *Neglecting to anchor the change in the organisational culture*: Unless new practices and behaviours are embedded in the culture of the organisation then the change will fail to 'stick'.

These causes of failure identified by Kotter can readily be mapped onto Lewin's three-stage model. These views of change encompass assumptions that change, because of its linearity, is a relatively straightforward process and that it can (and should) be driven from the top of the organisation and be implemented uniformly according to a detailed change plan. However, subsequent interpretation of Lewin's work challenges this simplistic view. In particular, a number of authors challenge the assumption of linearity and suggest that change may in reality be a more complex process. This view is shared by others, whose approaches entail educating mangers in a range of change theories, and involving them more actively in the change process by equipping them with practical tools Although seeing change as a more complex process this 'school' retains the assumption that change can be implanted uniformly throughout the organisation. However, this assumption of such a 'one-look' approach is widely challenged and empirical research has demonstrated that strategic-intent led change programmes often have unpredictable outcomes generated by interactions within the organisation. Similarly, a number of authors present empirical evidence demonstrating the failure of top-down change and the impact of unexpected or unintended outcomes resulting from interactions throughout the system.

Some have responded to these challenges to change models proposing an approach that, while retaining the assumption of linearity, recognises the need for a more distributed view of the nature of changes. Within this 'school' the general seat of change is set at the top of the organisation and agents throughout the organisation are equipped with a range of 'change tools' that they can determine how to use in pursuit of the overall direction.

In exploring the developments in arguments relating to change failure and approaches that overcome the challenges there appear to be two distinct schools of thought. These are:

- *Programmatic change*: this school of thought sees change as being a process of punctuated equilibrium; an organisation goes from one steady state, through a period of disruptive change and arrives at a new steady state. The characteristics of this approach tend to be:
  - Change is driven from the top and implemented uniformly throughout the organisation.
  - The approach to change is guided by linear thinking.
  - There is an assumption that there is inertia within the organisation and that people need to be encouraged to behave and think differently.
  - The role of the change leader is interventionist and needs to drive the change through the organisation.
  - The only goal of the change is one of enhancing economic value.

- *Emergent change*: this school of thought sees change as a natural part of the development and evolution of an organisation and views the organisation as a complex adaptive system. The characteristics of this approach tend to be:
  - Change is underpinned by systems thinking.
  - Change can start anywhere in the organisation; particularly at the edge or boundaries of the organisation.
  - There is an assumption that people are naturally self-organising and will readily take the initiative in identifying the need for change and implement new ways of working given the right conditions.
  - The role of the leader is one of facilitator and enabler of sensemaking in the organisation.

- Whilst the goal of the change contains an element of enhancing economic value it also includes one of building organisational capability.

Although these two world views are understood, in practice we have found that the programmatic approach tends to remain fairly dominant (particularly in relation to large-scale change). Overall change continues to be dominated by practice that embodies the following assumptions:

- change needs to be driven from the top of the organisation;
- approaches need to be carefully managed to deliver results; and
- clear, and relatively straightforward, programmes of actions need to be established.

It has been argued that much of the research into change and its success fails to consider different elements of change. These can be seen as being: context, content, and process. In more detail these are:

- *Context*: factors that relate to the organisation's external and internal environments such as changing competitive environments or the institutionalisation of a public organisation.
- *Content*: focuses on the content of the change that includes the organisation's strategies, structures and systems.
- *Process*: this element describes the interventions and processes that are involved in the implementation of change.

In broad terms most authors in the field tend to look at change from a relatively high level and both authors and researchers tend to pay limited attention to the process element of change. Furthermore, there is often little distinction between types of change that organisations face. There does appear to be an assumption that all types of change can be managed in the same way, or by applying a 'one-size-fits-all' model. However, it is clear that different types or scales of change entail different challenges and considerations. Kuipers and colleagues propose a useful typology that identifies different orders of change (Kuipers et al., 2014). These are:

- *First-order change*: This is change that impacts a sub-system in the organisation (e.g., a department, division). It tends to entail the adaptation of systems or structures and to be incremental and, often not overly disruptive.
- *Second-order change*: This order tends to impact a number of systems within the organisation. It often entails organisation-wide change and is frequently transformational in nature. As such it tends to be more disruptive than first order change.
- *Third-order change*: Change that goes across a number of organisations is referred to as third-order change. Often such change impacts all organisations within a sector. We tend to see many examples of such change within the public sector. In the private sector we tend to see change driven by new regulations or disruptive innovation within sub-sectors. In broad terms such change entails significant disruption; even total transformation of a sector.

From this categorisation of change, it is evident that the challenges will differ between different types of change being experienced.

In researching change there has been a dearth of studies that explore the *process* in detail. One notable exception to this was the study by Higgs and Rowland (2011) who set out to examine what processes and practices are encountered when organisations engage in change. They interviewed leaders from 20 organisations and each leader provided two change stories. In total they gathered around 100 such stories and subsequently analysed them. Leaders either saw change as:

- Straightforward, linear and predictable or complex and unpredictable.
- Something to be implemented in a consistent way throughout the organisation or something to be implemented in different ways in different parts of the organisation.

By analysing the stories in each category they identified four distinct approaches to implementing change. The characteristics of each approach, which appear to be related to the underlying mind-set informing the change approach, were:

- 'Directive' *Change* (mind-set: 'I can manage change.')
  - What has to be done is set top down and tightly controlled.
  - In terms of the 'how' of the change people have to follow prescribed steps and recipes.
  - People are provided with the same messages from the centre.
  - Change is driven through separate projects.
  - There is little, if any, investment in building change skills.
  - There is a requirement for 100% alignment—*'you're in or you're out'*.
  - Leaders say—*'keep it simple, just go do it'*.
  - People are engaged by informing them with the aim of getting 'buy in'.
- 'Self-Assembly' *Change* (mind-set: 'Launch enough initiatives and something will stick.')

  - There is centralised direction, with detail and accountability left to local management.
  - Standard tools and templates are handed out to the field for local implementation.
  - There is the adoption of a 'Pick 'n mix' approach— people can select what they need to do at local level.
  - The content of the change is defined; the process is up to local leaders.
  - Support teams and 'help desks' are set up to provide advice on how to implement the change.

- 'Master' *Change* (mind-set: 'I trust people to solve things with us'.)

  - What has to be done is set top down, tested with others, and open to adjustment.
  - Change is guided by a common plan, agreed projects and consistent language.
  - People are involved to sense what's going on and build their responsibility for figuring things out.
  - Effort is invested in building skills in leading change, including how to help people through it.
  - Networks are set up to build connections across the organisation.

- Effort is made to understand who is important for the change and to identify how to get and keep them on board.

- 'Emergent' *Change* (mind-set: 'I can only create the conditions for change to happen'.)

  - Within an overall purpose, the direction is adjusted as people make sense of what is needed.
  - Leaders establish a few 'big rules' that guide what people can do.
  - People can then get on with things as they see fit.
  - Initiatives start in a small way and build up from there
  - Informal networks are used to build understanding and energy.
  - People work step by step; there is no need to figure out the whole plan in advance
  - Leaders go to the 'hot spots' where things are bubbling up and draw people's attention to them.

Within this framework, they found that Directive change tended only to succeed where the change was internally driven and was, essentially, first-order change. Self-Assembly change was not found to be successful in any context. Master and Emergent change seemed to be successful across a range of contexts and, in particular, was successful in implementing second-order change. They drew this together in terms of understanding change in the context of complexity and asserted that:

- Change approaches that tend to be programmatic and rooted in a viewpoint, that see change initiatives as linear, sequential, and, consequently, predictable tended to fail in most contexts.
- Approaches that recognise change as a complex responsive process and embed this recognition within the overall change process tend to be successful across most contexts.

Overall, they concluded that:

Doing change **to** *people (i.e., Directive and Self Assembly) is likely to be unsuccessful, whereas doing change* **with** *people (i.e. Master and Emergent) is more likely to lead to successful implementation.*

Once again, this highlights an increasing need to develop leadership that adopts an engaging and facilitating style as well as taking account of the context.

4   Follower Commitment to Change

The high level of rates of change failure are rarely attributed to technical issues alone, more often they are asserted to result from human dynamics. Indeed, research on change management has often been criticised for neglecting the human dynamics of change. It has been argued that organisational failure to create readiness for change is one of the core reasons for the lack of success of many organisational change programmes. Hence, researchers have emphasised the importance of employees' reaction to change and their willingness to engage in the change as key success factors. Many see this as being related to the considerations of employee commitment. With this in mind more recent research has shifted towards investigating how employees' intentions to support and engage in organisational change initiatives are formed. In line with these arguments there is a case for integrating research into employee reactions to change and how these reactions impact on behaviour and commitment to the change.

The concept of commitment to change has been derived from the broader organisational commitment literature (outlined previously). Research into the link between leadership and organisational performance has shown that the leader plays an important role in this link and can have a strong impact on employee attitudes such as organisational commitment. Accordingly, leaders are critical for the implementation of change, and their behaviours are critical for employee satisfaction with them and with outcomes at the individual and organisational levels.

Until recently, little attention has been paid to the experiences and behaviours of leaders in the change process, and the impact of these behaviours on the success or failure of change. These studies have tended to explore both leader behaviours and change outcomes at the meso and micro levels. The relatively few studies that examine leadership impact on change have tended to examine the role and behaviours of top/senior leaders. However, within the broader leadership literature there is an increasing view that leadership is a more distributed function and that managers at all levels in the organisation can play a significant leadership role in change implementation. It is also suggested that the behaviours of leaders in change implementation will impact the behaviours and commitment of followers to the change. In particular, it has been pointed out that the framing of issues by leaders provides a structure that guides follower sensemaking. In a similar vein, the concept of authentic leadership is positioned as enabling followers to develop commitment to goals through the clarity and frame provided by the leader. This is seen to enable followers to develop their potential and contribute to goal achievement that, in turn, builds commitment to the change. It is evident that the principles of involvement and engagement, considered in the earlier broader discussion of employee commitment, apply even more significantly within the context of change. Furthermore, research has demonstrated that achieving high levels of employee commitment to change is essential for effective change implementation.

Given the emerging focus on the leaders' roles and behaviours in change, as a significant antecedent of success, we now turn to considering the area of leadership and change.

5   Leadership and Change

In exploring the leadership context we have suggested that there is a growing realisation that a major issue facing organisations is that of managing continuous change. Increasingly, organisations are facing the reality that the future is not one of incremental improvement or adjustment, but rather one of radical change or reinvention of the business. However, the evidence of organisations' ability to cope effectively with radical change is somewhat limited. To lead an organisation through such a change process takes considerable skill, ability and personal commitment.

Although much of the change literature examines the processual issues surrounding change implementation, there is a growing interest in the role of leadership in successful change implementation. Whilst the area of change leadership is really at its early stages of development, there is clear and growing evidence that the role of leaders in the change process does significantly affect the success of change. In the general leadership literature the beliefs and mind-sets of leaders have been shown to influence their orientation of choices and approaches to problem solving Thus, it may be implied that leaders' behaviours will influence their approach to change and its implementation. However, it has been asserted that the role and behaviours of leaders in a change context *per se* has been an area that is lacking in empirical research. The transformational leadership model Bass (1990) has been one that has been the subject of much empirical investigation (as discussed above). This stream of research does demonstrate clear linkages between leader behaviours and a variety of 'follower' behaviours and performance measures. However, this research generally fails to link directly with the change literature. Within the leadership literature, there have been criticisms that the predominantly quantitative approach fails to provide insights into the actual behaviours of leaders.

Perhaps the most dominant model of change leadership to date has been that proposed by Kotter (1995) who developed this from his work on causes of change failure. He proposed the following components of successful change leadership:

1. *Establishing a sense of urgency.* In essence, making the case for change and the need to act quickly.
2. *Forming a powerful coalition.* Ensuring that key players are working together to lead the change effort.
3. *Creating a vision.* Ensuring that a clear picture of the desired and possible future is established and an overall means of realising this vision is established.
4. *Communicating the vision.* Working actively to ensure that everyone in the organisation understands the new vision and the strategies for achieving it.
5. *Empowering others to act on the vision.* Having established and communicated the vision, working to enable others to contribute to its realisation and removing barriers to change. This entails encouraging new ways of behaving and rewarding those who respond to the challenge.

6. *Planning for creating short-term wins.* Ensuring that the results of actions that are in line with the vision are clearly visible and are planned to result in performance improvements. In addition ensuring that such actions and their results are publicised and visibly acknowledged.

7. *Consolidating improvements and producing still more change.* Building on the 'early wins' and their value to encourage greater effort to pursue the change goals. Publicly acknowledging and promoting those who are contributing to the new vision and to securing significant changes.

8. *Institutionalising new approaches.* Ensuring that all are aware of the relationship between new behaviours and the success of the organisation. Actively working to develop and promote those with the skills and abilities to engage others in the change process.

However, many have suggested that this view of change leadership remains at a relatively high descriptive level. This seems to be typical of studies and models that examine the leader's role and behaviour in the change process. Few studies have moved beyond generic descriptions. Exceptions to these are the studies reported by Higgs and Rowland who have specifically linked leadership behaviours to activities involved in implementing change. In an early study they identified five broad areas of leadership competency associated with successful change implementation:

1. *Creating the case for change*: Effectively engaging others in recognising the business need for change;

2. *Creating structural change*: Ensuring that the change is based on depth of understanding of the issues and supported with a consistent set of tools and processes;

3. *Engaging others* in the whole change process and building commitment;

4. *Implementing and sustaining changes*: Developing effective plans and ensuring good monitoring and review practices are developed; and

5. *Facilitating and developing capability*: Ensuring that people are challenged to find their own answers and that they are supported in doing this.

Furthermore, they found very strong linkages between these capabilities and elements of EI (discussed in earlier chapters). In exploring this work further, Higgs and Rowland (2005) studied specific leadership behaviours within some 70 change stories and their impact on change success in differing contexts. Their analyses identified three broad sets of leadership behaviour, which they categorised as:

1. *Shaping behaviour*: The communication and actions of leaders related directly to the change: 'making others accountable', 'thinking about change', and 'using an individual focus';
2. *Framing change*: Establishing starting points for change: 'designing and managing the journey' and 'communicating guiding principles in the organisation'; and
3. *Creating capacity*: Creating individual and organisational capabilities and communication and making connections.

From their analyses, they demonstrated that leader-centric behaviours (i.e., shaping) had a negative impact on change success in all the contexts examined. This finding tends to endorse the broader critique of the 'heroic' and leader-centric models that have dominated research in the leadership field. On the other hand, the more relational group- and systemic-focused behaviours (i.e., framing and creating) were related positively to change success in most of the contexts they examined. These findings tend to align with developments in the broader area of leadership studies. For example, Bartunek (1984) points out that the framing of issues by leaders provides a structure that guides follower sensemaking. In a similar vein, the concept of authentic leadership is positioned as enabling followers to develop commitment to goals through the clarity and frame provided by the leader. This is seen to enable followers to develop their potentiality and contribute to goal achievement. Furthermore, when Higgs and Rowland (2005) examined the relationship between leadership behaviours and change approaches, they found that 'shaping' behaviours tended to be more widely encountered within the more programmatic approaches to implementing change, whereas 'framing' and 'creating' were predominant behaviour sets in approaches that were based on the recognition of change as a complex phenomenon.

Furthermore, they identified that leaders who had a notable combination of the 'framing' and 'creating' behavioural sets appeared to be particularly successful in implementing change across most of the contexts examined.

In a follow up study with leaders in 33 organisations Higgs and Rowland (2005) used interviews to explore leadership behaviours and practices in more detail. These interview transcripts were coded employing a coding frame based on a combination of:

1. The broad categories of leadership behaviour identified in their earlier studies; and
2. A review of the emerging models from the leadership literature (see above) and the change leadership literature.

Based on this approach, the final coding frame encompassed their original leadership behaviour sets (i.e., shaping, framing and creating) together with four new categories that appeared to capture behaviours exhibited by leaders combining framing and creating. These new behaviour sets were described as being:

- *Attractor*: Creates a magnetic energy force in the organisation to pull it toward its purpose. The leaders pull people toward what the organisation is trying to do, not toward them.
- *Edge and tension*: The leader tests and challenges the organisation; amplifies the disturbance generated by the change process by helping people see the repeating and unhelpful patterns of behaviour in the culture while at the same time staying firm to keep the change process on course.
- *Container*: The leader holds and channels energy, which in unnerving times of change, provides calm, confident and affirming signals that allow people to find positive meaning and sense in an anxious situation.
- *Transforming space*: The leader creates change in the 'here and now' based on the assumption that the only thing you can change is the present moment.

In addition, they found continued presence of shaping behaviour.

When they analysed the impact of these new behaviours and practices on change success they found that leaders who exhibited all four of the new behaviours at a high level and minimal shaping behaviours were successful in implementing change across a broad range of contexts. They found that such a pattern of leadership behaviours and practices accounted for 50 % of the variation in change success. Thus, once again we see that leadership of change requires a move away from a heroic model to one of engaging and facilitating styles and behaviours.

6   Summary and Conclusion

In this chapter we have seen that our thinking about leadership needs to be set within a context of:

- complexity,
- commitment, and
- change.

The environment and context is one of volatility, uncertainty, complexity and ambiguity. The 'traditional' heroic leadership model is ill-fitted for this environment. There is a clear need for leaders to focus on developing a climate that engages employees and enables them to contribute and realise their potential. The need for this shift in focus is particularly critical in the arena of implementing change. Unless the shift happens then we will continue to face a situation in which 70 % of change initiatives fail.

We have seen evidence that this 'new Leadership' is underpinned by the EI of the leaders. However, it is hopefully clear that leaders also need the cognitive competencies to deal with the complex environment and the managerial competencies to assist in delivering results. Once again we might that effective leadership (that builds follower commitment) requires:

$$IQ + EQ + MQ$$

Perhaps we can best describe this as being Emotionally Intelligent Leadership. We will explore this idea in more detail in Chapter 8.

Bibliography

Allen, N. J., & Meyer, J. P. (1990). The measurement and antecedents of affective, continuance and normative commitment to the organization. *Journal of Occupational Psychology, 63*(1), 1–18.

Bartunek, J. M. (1984). Changing interpretive schemes and organizational restructuring: The example of a religious order. *Administrative Science Quarterly, 29*, 355–372.

Bass, B. M. (1990). *Bass and Stodghill handbook of leadership: Theory, research and applications.* New York, NY: Free Press.

Buchanan, D., & Boddy, D. (1992). *The expertise of the change agent.* London: Prentice Hall.

Blackmore, S. (1998). *The meme machine.* Oxford: Oxford University Press.

Higgs, M. J., & Rowland, D. (2005). All changes great and small: Exploring approaches to change and its leadership. *Change Management Journal, 5*(2), 121–151.

Higgs, M. J., & Rowland, D. (2011). What does it take to implement change successfully? A study of the behavior of successful change leaders. *Journal of Applied Behavioral Science, 47*(3), 309–335.

Kotter, J. P. (1995). Leading change: Why transformation efforts fail. *Harvard Business Review,* May–June, 11–16.

Kuipers, B. S., Higgs, M. J., Kickert, W. J. M., Tummers, L. G., Grandia, J., & Van der Voet, J. (2014). The management of change in public organisations: A literature review. *Public Administration, 92*(1), 1–20.

Lewin, K. (1951). *Field theory in social science.* New York: Harper & Row.

8

A Model of Emotionally Intelligent Leadership

1   Background

So far we have seen that:

* There is a link between EI and leadership.
* Effective leadership has been reconceptualised, moving away from the 'heroic' model to one that is facilitating and engaging.
* Leadership needs to be understood within the context in which organisations operate—particularly the contexts of complexity and change

It is this background that gives rise to the concept of emotionally intelligent leadership. This chapter describes how our research into EI and leaders' competencies have been applied to develop a framework for assessing an individual's leadership style within a context that aligns with the conclusions drawn from our reviews of the leadership literature. This provides the basis for our model of emotionally intelligent leadership.

© The Editor(s) (if applicable) and the Author(s) 2016
M. Higgs, V. Dulewicz, *Leading with Emotional Intelligence*,
DOI 10.1007/978-3-319-32637-5_8

2   Senior Managers' Emotional Intelligence and Leadership

Through our earlier research into EI, we identified that many elements of EI in our model of the construct also appeared in the models of others researching into, and writing about, the subject of leadership. In addition, our research on business leaders' (i.e., CEOs and general managers) competencies have identified a number of other cognitive (IQ) and managerial (MQ) competencies that are seen to be vital for business leadership. We start by reviewing some of our key findings.

In our early research, we reflected on a study of the achievement of general managers conducted by Victor Dulewicz and Peter Herbert (1999). This entailed using data from 100 general managers and their bosses who had assessed the former's performance using a personal competencies questionnaire, the Job Competencies Survey (JCS). In addition, participants had provided information about their job level and responsibilities. Seven years later, they were followed up, and asked for an update of their data on level and responsibility. Using a redefinition of EI in competency terms, together with the data from this follow-up study, we tested whether or not EI was able to predict long-term managerial advancement. Of the 40 competencies assessed, 16 appeared to cover the concept of EI. Performance on all of these competencies was aggregated into one measure that predicted, statistically significantly, the advancement of participants within their respective organisations over the seven-year period.

Recalling Daniel Goleman's (1996) basic proposition that 'EQ' and 'IQ' are both important for success, those competencies in the JCS questionnaire that were concerned with intellectual performance and cognitive competencies—IQ (12 in all) were also identified. An aggregate of these ratings of performance also predicted organisational advancement. After analysing the remaining 12 competencies in the JCS, it became clear that they were all essentially concerned with important aspects of management. To complete the picture, these were referred to as 'MQ' competencies, and examples of those rated highly important included: delegating/empowering, communicating, business sense, achievement motivation, motivating and developing others. An aggregate measure of MQ also predicted managerial advancement.

In order to explore the proportion of the total advancement figure explained by each of these three scales, a regression analysis was conducted. From this, it was found that the IQ competencies accounted for 27 % of the variance on advancement, quite close to Goleman's reported estimate from educational research of 20 %. EQ accounted for more than one-third of the variance (36 %) and finally, MQ explained 16 % of advancement. We concluded that EQ factors appear to be particularly important in explaining managerial success in the context of advancement. The core proposition suggested by Goleman, that IQ + EQ = Success, was supported. However, it was felt to be vital not to overlook other competencies that are more specifically related to the managerial task (i.e., MQ).

In a separate and unrelated study, Victor Dulewicz and Keith Gay (1997) investigated the competencies that are considered important for successful directors. A total of 338 directors took part in this study, drawn from the entire spectrum of UK companies, including representation from FTSE 100 corporate leaders. Of the 38 competencies under investigation, nine were identified as being closely linked to the elements of EI. These authors were particularly interested in two *corporate leadership* roles, the chairperson who is leader of the board and the chief executive who is leader of the company. Their results showed that, with only one exception (energy), *all* of the competencies that are closely aligned with the seven elements of EI were seen as being *vital* or *highly relevant* to these two *leadership* positions by the majority of directors.

Their results also confirmed that all of the IQ and MQ competencies were rated *vital* or *highly relevant* by a simple majority of CEOs, and the majority of competencies by at least two-thirds of those surveyed. Therefore, the outcome of these initial studies convinced us that the 'EQ, IQ and MQ' model also had a role in explaining top-level leadership within organisations. In order to conduct future research we developed a questionnaire that examined a combination of EQ, IQ and MQ. This was called *the Leadership Dimensions Questionnaire (LDQ)*.[1] Its development and use in our research is explored further in this chapter.

3   Links between Emotional Intelligence and Leadership

In the early days we had found that an increasing number of academics and practitioners were beginning to explore, accept or indeed promote the importance of EI at the top of the organisation. Examples of academics include the eminent organisational psychologists Warren Bennis (1989) in his book *On becoming a leader*, and Roger Gill (2001), then Professor of Leadership at Strathclyde University.

From a practitioner perspective, the importance of EI at senior and board level has been highlighted by many, including the then Director-General of the UK Institute of Directors Tim Melville-Ross, and the leading UK industrialist Sir John Egan, who was at the time President of the CBI and had formerly been CEO of Jaguar and BAA. Furthermore, in their book on EI and leadership, Daniel Goleman, Richard Boyatzis and Ann McKee (2002) claimed that:

> *Emotional Intelligence is twice as important as IQ and technical skills [...] The higher up the organisation you go, the more important emotional intelligence becomes.*

Given this we went on to explore whether or not this claim could be borne out by revisiting assessment data that were available on the personal competencies of 88 Directors, CEOs and Chairpersons. If Goleman and colleagues' claims were to hold, one would expect to find that Chairpersons and CEOs would have higher levels of EI than other directors. Using statistical tests to compare differences between the two groups, we found a significant difference on the EQ competencies and also a highly significant difference in terms of the IQ competencies, but no difference was found on the Managerial (MQ) competencies. A second exploratory study reanalysed data from the general managers' study mentioned above. Directors in the sample were found to have higher levels of EI than managers. This indeed provided some evidence to support the claims of Goleman and colleagues.

In looking more broadly at leadership and, in particular, the future nature of leadership, a number of authors and researchers at the time had identified the growing significance of EI. In part, this shift in focus from the rational to relational and emotional aspects of leadership represented the continuation of a trend encountered more broadly in thinking on organisational behaviour and leadership. Indeed, although not explicitly stated, according to Malcolm Higgs and Deborah Rowland (2001), much of the literature on transformational leadership implied that leaders require EI. Indeed, the more recent developments in authentic leadership suggest that the balance between self-awareness (EI) and other competencies are significant components of the construct.

3.1   Support for 'EQ, IQ and MQ' from the Leadership Literature

Our review of the leadership literature from the 'transformational' period onwards focused on models that contain clearly defined, behavioural constructs. On the basis of a content analysis of these constructs, there appears to be strong indications of a linkage between leadership and EI.

Building on Malcolm Higgs and Deborah Rowland's (2001) work, the authors went on to develop a 'map' of some of the key leadership models and their potential relationship to their elements of EI. The key themes were propounded by a range of researchers and authors on the subject of leadership and are presented in Table 8.1. From this analysis, it was clear that there were significant overlaps between aspects of leadership and respective elements of EQ.

The authors also conducted a similar mapping exercise on the key themes propounded by some researchers and authors onto the IQ and MQ dimensions they had identified as being required for effective leadership. Once again, they found a high degree of conceptual overlap, as shown in Table 8.2. In particular, the Bass and Avolio (1996) and Alimo-Metcalf and Alban-Metcalf (2005) models provided support for all eight IQ and MQ dimensions. However, the other models all provided links with at least five of the eight IQ and MQ dimensions. The results of these mapping exercises provide strong evidence to support the content validity of the LDQ questionnaire.

Table 8.1 Relationships between leadership 'models' and EQ dimensions

Elements of emotional intelligence (Higgs & Dulewicz, 2002)	Leadership models and frameworks						
	Bass and Avolio (1996)—MLQ Transactional/transformational	Alimo-Metcalfe and Alban-Metcalfe(2005)—TLQ	Goffee and Jones (2000) Four Factors	Kouznes and Posner (1998)	Kotter (1990)—What leaders do	Bennis (1989)	Goleman et al. (2002)
Self-awareness		• Self-awareness	• Reveal differences • Selectively show weaknesses			• Develop self-knowledge • Develop feedback sources	• Pacesetting
Emotional resilience	Fixes problems		• Tough empathy	• Challenges processes • Enable others		• Balance change a transition • Learn from adversity	
Motivation	• Charismatic leadership • Objective setting • Focus on performance	• Determined	• Tough empathy	• Challenge processes • Model the way	• Motivating and inspiring • Setting directions	• Role model	• Pacesetting • Commanding

Interpersonal sensitivity	• Individual consideration • Charismatic leadership • Intellectual stimulation • Provide support and feedback	• Genuine concern • Sensitive change management	• Tough empathy • Selectively show weaknesses	• Challenge processes • Inspire shared vision • Enable others • Model the way • Encourage the heart	• Aligning people	• Open style	• Affiliative • Democratic
Influence	• Charismatic leadership • Individual consideration		• Reveal differences • Tough empathy	• Inspire shared vision • Enable others	• Aligning people • Motivating and inspiring • Setting direction	• Open style	• Affiliative • Democratic • Coaching
Intuitiveness	• Intellectual stimulation	• Decisive	• Intuition	• Inspire shared vision • Encourage the heart		• Capacity to concentrate • Curious about innovation	
Conscientiousness and integrity	• Individual consideration	• Integrity • Transparency	• Tough empathy • Reveal differences	• Model the way • Encourage the heart	• Aligning people	• Role model	

Table 8.2 Relationships between leadership 'models' and IQ and MQ dimensions

Dimensions of intellectual & managerial	Leadership models and frameworks						
	Bass and Avolio (1996)—MLQ Transactional/ transformational	Alimo-Metcalfe and Alban-Metcalfe (2005)—TLQ	Goffee and Jones (2000) Four factors	Kouznes and Posner (1998)	Kotter (1990)—What leaders do	Bennis (1989)	Goleman et al. (2002) New leaders
Critical analysis & judgement	• Intellectual stimulation • Fixes problems	• Encourages critical thinking		• Challenging the process			
Vision & imagination	• Intellectual stimulation	• Shared vision	• Intuitive	• Inspires shared vision	• Motivating and inspiring	• Curious about innovation	• Visionary
Strategic perspective	• Intellectual stimulation	• Manages change sensitively • Intellectual versatility	• Intuitive	• Inspires shared vision		• Curious about innovation	• Visionary
Engaging communication	• Charismatic, inspirational • Focus on performance	• Inspirational communicator • Charismatic	• Selectively show weaknesses	• Model the way	• Motivating and inspiring	• Open style	
Managing resources	• Planning • Organising • Develop clear objectives and expectations • Provide feedback	• Clarifies direction and purpose			• Setting direction	• Balance change and transition	• Commanding

Empowering	• Intellectual stimulation • Participative decision-making • Provide support • Provide feedback	• Empowering		• Enable others to act	• Aligning people	• Open style • Democratic
Developing	• Participative decision-making • Provide support • Provide feedback	• Creates learning culture	• Tough empathy	• Enable others to act	• Aligning people	• Open style • Coaching
Achieving	• Focus on performance • Contingent reward	• Decisive and determined	• Intuitive			• Pacesetting • Commanding

3.2   Recent Developments in Leadership Theory

Since the original work on the development of the LDQ, there have been notable developments in research and conceptualisation of leadership that are, indeed, supportive of the earlier work and tend to provide further support for the content validity of LDQ. In particular, the developments in the articulation of the concept of 'authentic leadership' and change leadership tend to endorse both the components of the LDQ and the significance of the change context. The components of 'authentic leadership' are:

- Self-awareness
- Balanced processing (emotional and rational)
- Strong moral compass
- Relational transparency
- Environmental scanning

These elements relate clearly to LDQ components of IQ, EQ and MQ.

In their early work on change leadership, Malcolm Higgs and Deborah Rowland (2005) identified the importance of the change context in determining the appropriate leadership style and behaviour. However, they did point out that a highly directive, leader-centric style of behaviour tends to have a negative impact on outcomes in many change contexts. They concluded that an engaging and facilitating leadership style tends to be effective in most change contexts. However, they point out that the way in which this is enacted differs and is based on the significance, magnitude and extent of the change. This provides further support for the style: context differences that are embedded within the LDQ and described below.

4   The Leadership Dimensions Questionnaire (LDQ)

The development of the LDQ is presented in detail in the LDQ Manual[2] in which we describe two pilot studies of the new LDQ. Data are presented on two-item analyses and on the reliability and validity of the final instrument which was piloted on 222 managers. Cronbach Alpha reliability coefficients were calculated for the cluster of items constituting each dimension, showing that all 15 LDQ scales are reliable.

4.1 Definitions of the LDQ Dimensions

On the basis of our studies just described and their detailed review of the leadership literature, we identified eight dimensions related to IQ and MQ competencies to add to the seven EQ dimensions defined in Chapter 3, in order to produce a framework to capture the main dimensions of effective leadership. Brief definitions of the eight IQ and MQ dimensions that emerged from this work are shown in Table 8.3.

Table 8.3 Definitions of the IQ and MQ dimensions of the LDQ

Intellectual dimensions (IQ)
Critical analysis and judgement
A critical faculty that probes the facts, identifies advantages and disadvantages and discerns the shortcomings of ideas and proposals. Makes sound judgments and decisions based on reasonable assumptions and factual information, and is aware of the impact of any assumptions made.

Vision and imagination
Imaginative and innovative in all aspects of one's work. Establishes sound priorities for future work. A clear vision of the future direction of the organisation to meet business imperatives. Foresees the impact of external and internal changes on one's vision that reflect implementation issues and business realities.

Strategic perspective
Sees the wider issues and broader implications. Explores a wide range of relationships, balances short- and long-term considerations. Sensitive to the impact of one's actions and decisions across the organisation. Identifies opportunities and threats. Sensitive to stakeholders' need, external developments and the implications of external factors on one's decisions and actions.

Managerial dimensions (MQ)
Resource management
Plans ahead, organises all resources and co-ordinates them efficiently and effectively. Establishes clear objectives. Converts long-term goals into action plans. Monitors and evaluates staff's work regularly and effectively, and gives them sensitive and honest feedback.

(continued)

Table 8.3 (continued)

Engaging communication
A lively and enthusiastic communicator, engages others and wins support.
  Clearly communicates instructions and vision to staff. Communications are
  tailored to the audience's interests and are focused. Approach inspires staff
  and audiences. Communication style conveys approachability and
  accessibility.

Empowering
Knows own direct report's strengths and weaknesses. Gives them
  autonomy, encourages them to take on personally challenging and
  demanding tasks. Encourages them to solve problems, produce innovative
  ideas and proposals and develop their vision for their area and a broader
  vision for the business. Encourages a critical faculty and a broad perspective,
  and encourages the challenging of existing practices, assumptions and
  policies.

Developing
Believes others have potential to take on ever more-demanding tasks and
  roles, and encourages them to do so. Ensures direct reports have adequate
  support. Develops their competencies, and invests time and effort in
  coaching them so they can contribute effectively and develop themselves.
  Identifies new tasks and roles that will develop others. Believes that critical
  feedback and challenge are important.

Achieving
Willing to make decisions involving significant risk to gain a business
  advantage. Decisions are based on core business issues and their likely
  impact on success. Selects and exploits activities that result in the greatest
  benefits to the organisation and that will increase its performance.
  Unwavering determination to achieve objectives and implement
  decisions.

4.2   The LDQ Leadership Model

The roots of the LDQ Model lie in the authors' original EI model. There
is much evidence from the literature to suggest that each of the elements
contributes to managerial performance. But how do they relate to each
other, so that the whole is greater than the sum of the parts? The relevant literature, covering competency and personality theory, and Freud's
work, with his model of the Id, the Ego and the Super-ego, was reviewed.
In particular, the conflict between the Ego (our consciousness) and the

Super-Ego (our conscience) and the need for balance in order to achieve maturity seemed relevant. The initial model of EI devised by the authors and shown in Chapter 4 had three main components:

1. *The driver* is motivation. This trait energises people and drives them towards achieving their goals, which are usually set very high.
2. *The constrainer*, high conscientiousness, on the other hand, can act as a control, and curbs the excesses of the driver, especially if they are very high and undirected, or misdirected.
3. *The enablers*, Self-awareness, emotional resilience, inter-personal sensitivity, influence and intuitiveness, are those traits that facilitate performance and help the individual to achieve targets or succeed in life generally.

The authors decided later that Reuven Bar-On's (1997) distinction between inter- and intra-personal elements/components is an important one, especially for research into managerial performance because inter-personal elements are paramount if managers are to achieve results with or through colleagues. Therefore, this distinction was added the original EI model.

From our research we posited that high performance should result, firstly, if the individual has high scores on all seven elements of EI— they are all contributing when in balance; or secondly, if all scores are average or above, and there are no large disparities between drivers and constrainers. On the other hand, low performance should result firstly, if scores are below-average on all seven elements; *or* secondly if overall EI, and the enablers scores are average, but the driver is high and the constrainer low, or vice-versa. In these cases, there would be imbalance. We tested this model empirically and the results were found to support it.

4.3   A Revised Model for LDQ

The revision to the EIQ model, incorporating the distinction between inter- and intra-personal elements and the IQ and MQ dimensions, is presented below:

Model components	LDQ dimension
Drivers	Motivation
	Achieving
Constrainer	Conscientiousness
Intra-personal enablers	Critical analysis
	Vision and imagination
	Strategic perspective
	Self-awareness
	Emotional resilience
	Intuitiveness
Inter-personal enablers	Engaging communication
	Managing resources
	Empowering
	Developing
	Interpersonal sensitivity
	Influence

A schematic representation of this revised model appears in Fig. 8.1. This clearly differentiates between inter- and intra-personal elements and also reflects the importance of the inter-personal enablers to the link with performance, the other elements being channelled through these two.

5   The Three Leadership Styles

Based on our earlier work (see Chapter 6) we suggest that effective leadership is increasingly being seen in terms of a combination of:

1. Personal characteristics that are required to enable an individual to engage in a leadership role in an effective manner;
2. A range of skills and behaviours that need to be in place to provide effective leadership;
3. A range of styles related to the context in which leadership is exercised;
4. A range of ways in which the leadership behaviours may be exercised in a way that matches the personal style of the individual leader.

In addition, it is quite widely accepted that leadership may be exhibited at many levels in an organisation.

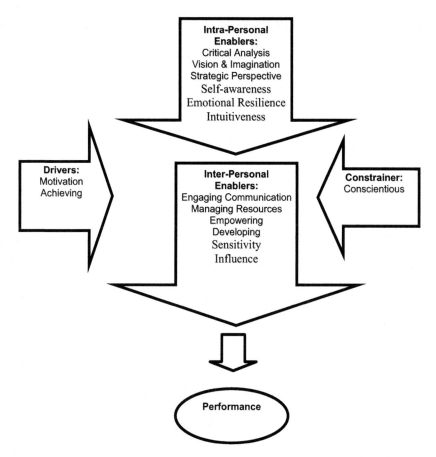

Fig. 8.1   The LDQ emotionally intelligent leadership model

Based on our review of the literature covering different leader behaviours in different contexts of change, the authors identified three distinct leadership styles:

1. *Engaging leadership.* A style based on a high level of empowerment and involvement appropriate in a highly transformational context in which the organisation is facing radical change that impacts many aspects of the business. Such a style is focused on producing radical change with high levels of engagement and commitment.

2. *Involving leadership.* A style that is based on a transitional context in which the organisation that faces significant, but not necessarily radical, changes in its business model or *modus operandi*. Having said this, it may be that within any sub-system some element of radical change may be required. However, the core business model remains unchanged.
3. *Goal leadership.* A style that is focused on delivering results within a relatively stable context. This is a leader-led style aligned to a stable organisation delivering clearly understood results. This is not to say that no change is involved. It may be that incremental adjustment may be taking place in a number of aspects of the business but there are like to be peripheral to the core business model.

The profile for each style, based upon the range (high, medium or low) of scores obtained on the 15 LDQ dimensions, is presented in Table 8.4. These profiles were developed from a content analysis of the literature on leadership and change. Initially, this focused on the transformational and transactional behaviours (Higgs & Rowland, 2001) that were context-based and subsequently expanded to encompass the change leadership and broader change literature. The *engaging style* was informed by authors

Table 8.4 Three leadership style profiles: Goal-oriented (G), Engaging (E) and Involving (I)

LDQ dimension	Low	Medium	High
Critical analysis and judgement		E I	G
Vision and imagination		E	G I
Strategic perspective		E I	G
Engaging communication		G I	E
Managing resources	E	I	G
Empowering	G	I	E
Developing		G I	E
Achieving		E I	G
Self-awareness		G	E I
Emotional resilience			G E I
Motivation			G E I
Interpersonal sensitivity		G I	E
Influencing		G	E I
Intuitiveness		G I	E
Conscientiousness			G E I

working in the transformational and change leadership fields. The traditional and the transactional leadership literature informed the development of the *goal-oriented style*. The *involving style* was again informed by both the more traditional leadership and change leadership literature.

We conducted some preliminary analyses of the leadership styles, using a 'closeness of fit' score (covering 64 % of the total pilot sample of 222). This showed that all three styles were fairly well represented within the sample. Almost one-third (31 %) had a predominantly Goal-oriented style; 28 % had an Involving style and 41 % had an Engaging style. Furthermore, this breakdown did not vary according to the gender, sector (public/private), function or nationality of the manager.

Further analyses looked at the personality characteristics (from the 16PF personality questionnaire) of those well fitted to each style. All three styles have a number of extravert personality factors in common, as well as being tough and forthright. Turning to style-specific characteristics, those with an Engaging style tend to be emotionally well-adjusted extraverts while those who are 'goal-oriented' are more likely to be conscientious.

5.1 Organisational Context

As noted Chapter 7, the context within which leaders operate is a major factor mediating their performance. From the literature review, we concluded that the different styles, matched to the degree of contextual volatility, would be important in determining both appropriateness and effectiveness. Therefore, an Organisational Context scale was designed (Part II of the LDQ) to examine the degree and nature of change and volatility in their working environment that respondents perceive they face in their role as a leader. After trials, the final scale, developed to assess the leadership context, consists of 21 items relating to various aspects of change being faced by the respondent. Analysis showed that the scale is made up of five separate factors:

- a general fundamental need to change;
- fundamental change of the organisation/business;
- the need for followers to change;

- specific pressures from the business environment; and
- an unstable context.

The 21 items in the final overall scale proved to be highly reliable.

5.2   Interpreting the Style Profiles

The higher the score on the Organisational Context scale, the greater the degree of volatility and change in the context in which individuals exercise leadership. There are three broad categories reflecting different contexts: relatively stable, significant change and transformational change.

The *LDQ report*[3] encourages participants to match their predominant leadership style to the context in which they are leading. In their reports, the respondents' LDQ Context score is presented, reflecting the degree of change they perceive that their organisation is facing. They are urged to review the leadership profile chart produced for that particular style and to examine the descriptions of each of the dimensions to determine which may need developing or exploiting so that they might be more effective in the appropriate style.

When reflecting on an individual's development needs, the final section of the report provides a detailed review of their scores on all 15 dimensions. The other two profiles are presented in case they are on the borderline of two different styles or feel that they might be required to adopt a different style in the foreseeable future.

6   Leadership Performance and Follower Commitment Scales

The second part of the LDQ also includes two other scales, which are designed for research purposes exclusively. No reference is made to these scores in the LDQ report. The first provides a self-assessment of leadership performance. It contains six items and is reliable. The other scale assesses the degree of commitment that followers show to the organisation and team in which they work, a construct that includes job satisfaction. It contains five items and is also reliable. Further details on the use of these scales for research appear in the LDQ Manual.

7   Summary and Conclusion

In this chapter we have described the development of a model of EI leadership and a related leadership questionnaire (LDQ) from our original Emotional Intelligence Questionnaire as well as the developments in leadership thinking and the need to consider leadership within a context of change. The model includes the original seven dimensions from the EIQ plus eight new dimensions measuring IQ and MQ. We went on to present a new overall model of leadership, before going on to describe three leadership styles derived from scores on the 15 LDQ dimensions. Finally, we noted the importance of context to determine which style is appropriate to a specific organisational context. This is the unique selling point of the LDQ, a facility not available from any other leadership questionnaire known to us. In the next chapter (Chapter 9) we move on to examine how EI leadership competencies and styles can be developed and illustrate this using examples and case studies.

Notes

1. The Leadership Dimensions Questionnaire (LDQ) is an assessment tool that is developed from the authors' work. It is published by VDA Assessment & Development Consultants.
2. See *The LDQ Technical Manual* published by VDA Assessment & Development Consultants.
3. The Leadership Dimensions Questionnaire (LDQ) is also used in research, see the LDQ Manual (note 2 this chapter) for details.

Bibliography

Alimo-Metcalfe, B., & Alban-Metcalfe, J. (2005). Leadership: Time for a new direction? *Leadership, 1*(1), 51–71.

Bar-On, R. (1997). *Bar-On Emotional Quotient Inventory (EQ-i): Technical manual.* Toronto: Multi-Health Systems.

Bass, B. M., & Avolio, B. J. (1996). *Postscripts: Recent developments for improving organisational effectiveness.* London: Sage.

Bennis, W. (1989). *On becoming a leader.* London: Hutchinson.

Dulewicz, V., & Gay, K. (1997). Personal competences for board directors: The main dimensions and role comparisons. *Competency Journal, 4*(3), 37–44.

Dulewicz, V., & Herbert, P. J. A. (1999). Predicting advancement to senior management from competencies and personality data: A 7-year follow-up study. *British Journal of Management, 10*(1), 13–22.

Gill, R. (2001). Change management or change leadership? *Journal of Change Management, 3*, 307–318.

Goffee, R., & Jones, G. (2000). Why should anyone be led by you? *Harvard Business Review,* September–October, 63–70.

Goleman, D. (1996). *Emotional intelligence: Why it can matter more than IQ.* New York: Bantam Books.

Goleman, D., Boyatzis, R. E., & McKee, A. (2002). *Primal leadership: Realizing the power of emotional intelligence.* Boston, MA: Harvard Business School Press.

Higgs, M. J., & Dulewicz, V. (2002). *Making sense of emotional intelligence* (2nd ed.). London: ASE Test Publishing.

Higgs, M. J., & Rowland, D. (2001). Developing change leaders: Assessing the impact of a development programme. *Change Management Journal, 2*(1), 25–36.

Higgs, M. J., & Rowland, D. (2005). All changes great and small: Exploring approaches to change and its leadership. *Change Management Journal, 5*(2), 121–151.

Kotter, J. P. (1990). *A force for change: How leadership differs from management.* New York: Simon & Schuster.

Kouzes, J. R., & Posner, B. F. (1998). *Encouraging the heart.* San Francisco, CA: Jossey-Bass.

9

Developing Emotionally Intelligent Leadership

1   Introduction

In Chapter 6 we outlined the way in which our thinking about the nature of effective leadership has developed. We argue that, in today's volatile, uncertain, complex and ambiguous environment, we need to think about leadership as a relational process that engages people and facilitates them in realising their potential and contributing to the goals of the organisation. Furthermore, we suggested that within this framework leaders require strong levels of EI. We presented evidence to support this assertion, based on a range of empirical studies.[1] Based on the developments in leadership thinking and a review of the leadership context (see Chapter 6) an engaging and facilitating approach to leadership requires a combination of emotional intelligence (EQ), cognitive competencies (IQ) and managerial competencies (MQ). Thus we proposed that:

Emotionally Intelligent Leadership = EQ + IQ + MQ

Indeed this proposed relationship is embedded in the model of emotionally intelligent leadership that is explored in Chapter 8. This is incorporated in the Leadership Dimensions Questionnaire[2] that is described in the chapter along with the empirical evidence that underpins it.

© The Editor(s) (if applicable) and the Author(s) 2016   **149**
M. Higgs, V. Dulewicz, *Leading with Emotional Intelligence*,
DOI 10.1007/978-3-319-32637-5_9

The question now arises as to how Emotionally Intelligent Leadership might be developed. To an extent we have looked at one aspect of this in 'Developing Emotionally Intelligent Leadership' (Chapter 5). We now turn to considering how the overall components of our emotionally intelligent leadership model might be developed.

2   A Development Framework

In proposing a development framework we suggest a number of steps that follow a similar route to the framework outline for the development of EI (Chapter 5). This framework is summarised in Fig. 9.1. We will now explore these steps in more detail.

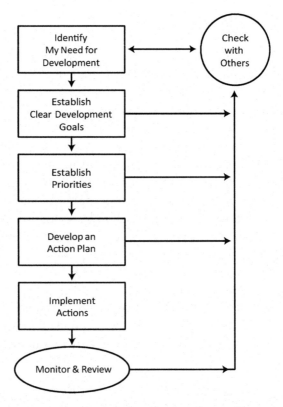

Fig. 9.1   Development framework for emotionally intelligent leadership

2.1   Step 1. Identify the Change Context

In developing emotionally intelligent leadership the first step is to consider the context within which leadership needs to be enacted. As is discussed in Chapter 7 one of the most significant contexts that impact on leadership relates to the extent of change being faced by the organisation. In Chapter 7 we identified the following broad change contexts that need to be considered when planning leadership development:

1. *Relatively stable*: This context arises when the organisation is not facing any significant changes to established ways of working or core principles. This is not to say that there is no change occurring. Rather there may well be incremental shifts in operations or practices that may relate to adaptations and continuous improvement as a part of 'business as usual'. Such incremental changes tend to impact on relatively small parts of the overall organisation's operations.
2. *Significant change*: Within this context the organisation, or major aspects of the organisation's work, face significant changes to systems, processes or operational practices. Such change tends to be disruptive and disturbs the existing ways of working.
3. *Transformational change*: Transformational change has a major impact on the organisation. It often entails changes to many parts of the organisation and its systems and processes. It often entails a major change to the organisations core business or operational model. It is the type of change that leads to significant disruption within the organisation.

The starting point in development planning is to consider the nature of the change context in your part of the organisation, reflecting on the above distinctions. If you have completed the LDQ you will have a good indication of the change context from your responses. However, as development will entail time and effort, it is important to reflect on your assessment in light of any organisational changes. It is also important to consider changes that your part of the organisation may face in the near future. For example, if the organisation has announced a new strategy it is likely that the change context will become more significant when it is implemented.

Case Example: Identifying the Context

We were working with the top team of a government agency responsible for managing safety in relation to major engineering projects and operations. The CEO perceived the change context as being a relatively stable one and the only changes being faced related to government budget reductions and enhanced reporting requirements.

In a meeting with his team the CEO was surprised to learn that his direct reports saw the budgetary and reporting changes as having a significant impact on the operations of the organisation. Furthermore, in the course of the discussion with the team it became apparent that the government's proposals to introduce competition into the provision of the core safety services would have a dramatic impact on the business operations, systems and processes. In the course of the discussion the team and CEO agreed that they would be facing transformational change in the near future.

In considering the context it is important to consider how your direct reports might be experiencing the change in addition to your own views. What you see as relatively stable your direct reports may see as being significant change. If you have completed an LDQ 360°[3] you will have some indication of the degree of agreement on the change context. If you have not used this tool (or even if you have) it is important to discuss the change context with your immediate team. Again, consider both the current situation and the implications of any new initiatives or external developments that may impact your change context. As the context is important for the planning of your development this is an important step (particularly ensuring that you understand how your direct reports perceive the context). This can be illustrated by considering a case that we have recently been involved with in a consulting assignment. This brief example provided shows that, for the CEO, the context to frame his leadership development planning really needed to be a *transformational* one.

2.2   Step 2. Review Style Fit Profiles

The emotionally intelligent leadership model identifies distinct leadership styles that are associated with each context. These relate to the 15 components identified in Chapter 8, identifying them as:

1. *Engaging leadership.* A style based on a high level of empowerment and involvement appropriate in a *highly transformational context.* Such a style is focused on producing radical change with high levels of engagement and commitment.
2. *Goal leadership.* A style focused on delivering results within a *relatively stable context.* This is a leader-led style aligned to a stable organisation delivering clearly understood results.
3. *Involving leadership.* A style based on a transitional organisation that faces *significant,* but not necessarily *radical changes* in its business model or modus operandi.

The LDQ provides feedback against these styles. Table 9.1 summarises these profiles.

In Table 9.1 'high' refers to a strong need for the capability, 'medium' to an average need and 'low' to a below average need for the capability. An example of the full profiles provided by the LDQ is provided in the sample report in Appendix A.

Table 9.1 LDQ style profiles

	Goal-oriented	Involving	Enabling
Personal Enablers			
Critical analysis and judgement	High	Medium	Medium
Vision and imagination	High	High	Medium
Strategic perspective	High	Medium	Medium
Managing resources	High	Medium	Low
Self-awareness	Medium	High	High
Emotional resilience	High	High	High
Intuitiveness	Medium	Medium	High
Interpersonal Enablers			
Interpersonal sensitivity	Medium	Medium	High
Influence	Medium	High	High
Engaging communication	Medium	Medium	High
Empowering	Low	Medium	High
Developing	Medium	Medium	High
Drivers			
Motivation	High	High	High
Achieving	High	Medium	Medium
Constrainer			
Conscientiousness	High	High	High

Having determined the context that you will be leading within you can now determine the target profile in order to be effective in that context. Again the relationship between the context and target profile is illustrated by the case outlined below.

Case Example: Identifying the Target Leadership Style
The CEO's original assessment of the organisation context (relatively stable) would have indicated a goal-oriented style. The initial discussion with the team indicated that the context should be seen as one of significant change requiring an involving style. However, the realisation that the forthcoming introduction, by the government, of competition leads to a transformational context, which requires an enabling style. Given the relatively near term of this major development the CEO determined that he should target his development on moving towards an enabling style.

2.3   Step 3. Assessing Your Own Profile Against the 'Best Fit' Profile

Having identified your target leadership style the next step is to identify where you are in relation to the 15 dimensions of the emotionally intelligent leadership model. Ideally, the best way to do this is to undertake a structured assessment using the LDQ instrument. However, as we did with the EI dimensions (see Chapter 5), we have proposed a brief framework to enable you to make a tentative initial assessment of your profile. This framework is shown in Table 9.2. In making your assessment you can rate yourself on a 1–10 scale, where 1 represents a relative lack of capability in relation to the dimension and 10 equates to a very high capability in relation to the dimension. To map this onto the required profile a high rating would be a score between 7 and 10, a medium would be a score of 5–6 and a low rating would be a score of between 1 and 4.

One way of enhancing the initial view of your own assessment is to discuss your views with your team of direct reports. The analysis helps you to identify those areas where you do need to undertake development action in order to move towards the appropriate style for your organisational context.

Table 9.2 Initial assessment of 15 dimensions of emotionally intelligent leadership

Dimension	Own rating	Target profile level
Personal Enablers		

Critical analysis and judgement
A critical faculty that probes the facts, identifies advantages and disadvantages and discerns the shortcomings of ideas and proposals. Makes sound judgments and decisions based on reasonable assumptions and factual information, and is aware of the impact of any assumptions made.

Vision and imagination
Imaginative and innovative in all aspects of one's work. Establishes sound priorities for future work. A clear vision of the future direction of the organisation to meet business imperatives. Foresees the impact of external and internal changes on one's vision that reflect implementation issues and business realities.

Strategic perspective
Sees the wider issues and broader implications. Explores a wide range of relationships, balances short- and long-term considerations. Sensitive to the impact of one's actions and decisions across the organisation. Identifies opportunities and threats. Sensitive to stakeholders' need, external developments and the implications of external factors on one's decisions and actions.

Resource management
Plans ahead, organises all resources and co-ordinates them efficiently and effectively. Establishes clear objectives. Converts long-term goals into action plans. Monitors and evaluates staff's work regularly and effectively, and gives them sensitive and honest feedback.

Self-awareness
Awareness of one's own feelings and the capability to recognise and manage these in a way that one feels that one can control. A degree of self-belief in one's capability to manage one's emotions and to control their impact in a work environment.

Emotional resilience
Performs consistently in a range of situations under pressure and adapts behaviour appropriately. Balances the needs of the situation and task with the needs and concerns of the individuals involved. Retains focus on a course of action or need for results in the face of personal challenge or criticism.

(*continued*)

Table 9.2   (continued)

Dimension	Own rating	Target profile level

Intuitiveness
Arrives at clear decisions and drives their implementation
  when presented with incomplete or ambiguous
  information using both rational and 'emotional' or
  intuitive perceptions of key issues and implications.

Interpersonal Enablers
Interpersonal sensitivity
Is aware of, and takes account of, the needs and perceptions
  of others in arriving at decisions and proposing solutions to
  problems and challenges. Builds from this awareness and
  achieves the commitment of others to decisions and action.
  A willingness to keep open one's thoughts on possible
  solutions to problems and to actively listen to, and reflect
  on, the reactions and inputs from others.

Influence
Persuades others to change views based on an
  understanding of their position and a recognition of the
  need to listen to this perspective and provide a rationale
  for change.

Engaging communication
A lively and enthusiastic communicator, engages others and
  wins support. Clearly communicates instructions and vision
  to staff. Communications are tailored to the audience's
  interests and are focused. Approach inspires staff and
  audiences. Communication style conveys approachability
  and accessibility.

Empowering
Knows own direct report's strengths and weaknesses. Gives
  them autonomy, encourages them to take on personally
  challenging and demanding tasks. Encourages them to
  solve problems, produce innovative ideas and proposals
  and develop their vision for their area and a broader vision
  for the business. Encourages a critical faculty and a broad
  perspective, and encourages the challenging of existing
  practices, assumptions and policies.

Table 9.2 (continued)

Dimension	Own rating	Target profile level
Developing		
Believes others have potential to take on ever more-demanding tasks and roles, and encourages them to do so. Ensures direct reports have adequate support. Develops their competencies, and invests time and effort in coaching them so they can contribute effectively and develop themselves. Identifies new tasks and roles that will develop others. Believes that critical feedback and challenge are important.		
Drivers		
Motivation		
Has the drive and energy to achieve clear results and make an impact and, also, to balance short- and long-term goals with a capability to pursue demanding goals in the face of rejection or questioning.		
Achieving		
Willing to make decisions involving significant risk to gain a business advantage. Decisions are based on core business issues and their likely impact on success. Selects and exploits activities that result in the greatest benefits to the organisation and that will increase its performance. Unwavering determination to achieve objectives and implement decisions.		
Constrainer		
Conscientiousness		
Displays clear commitment to a course of action in the face of challenge and to match 'words and deeds' in encouraging others to support the chosen direction. Shows personal commitment to pursuing an ethical solution to a difficult business issue or problem.		

What is evident from the target profiles is that in certain cases it is possible to display 'too much' of a capability. This is generally unlike the review of your EI that we explored in Chapter 4. With EI there is a general view that you should develop all elements to the highest possible level. However, even with EI there can be contexts in which too much presence of an element can be problematic. For example, in a study we conducted into the performance of call centre staff we found that high levels of intuitiveness were related negatively to performance. On further investigation this was found to be a problem due to the need to have complete and unambiguous information in order to follow the algorithms that underpinned the call centre agents' decisions. With the leadership profiles it is clear that exhibiting too high a focus on some dimensions reduces the match to the style needs. This arises particularly in relation to the following dimensions:

- Critical analysis and judgement
- Vision and imagination
- Strategic perspective
- Managing resources
- Achieving

In general, these become less important as the needed style moves away from goal-oriented. If faced with this situation it is clear that you cannot possess less of each dimension (nor should you). However, it is important to hold back somewhat from your natural tendencies when enacting a different style. Broadly the changes in behaviour in these circumstances entail a higher level of involving others and encouraging them to participate in the decision-making process. Table 9.3 provides some thoughts on actions you might take if you find that your target profile requires the reduction of your use of these elements.

The ideas outlined in Table 9.3 are by no means the only actions that can be taken to reduce the impact of higher levels of strength in these elements of leadership. You will no doubt think of other actions that can be helpful. The important point to bear in mind in thinking about these is that you will need to work to devolve more accountability for decisions and actions and to involve your team in these rather than use your capability on an exclusive basis.

The assessment process in action can again be illustrated with reference to the case that we have been considering.

Case Example: Assessing Your Own Profile against 'Best-Fit' Style
As we have seen above the CEO originally saw the context he was in as being relatively stable and requiring a goal-oriented style. However, based on discussions with his team he realised that the context was transformational and the 'best-fit' style was an engaging one.
Below is the profile analysis for the CEO against that style.

Table 9.3   Reducing the impact of high levels of leadership elements

Element	Actions to reduce the impact of the element
Critical analysis and judgement	• Encourage team members to critique arguments and proposals • Encourage team members to think about and make explicit their assumptions in making and reviewing proposals and decisions • Encourage team members to propose solutions to problems that arise and assess the strengths and weaknesses of their proposals • Discuss proposals, problems and issues with the team and seek their input rather than presenting your ideas
Vision and imagination	• Actively involve team members in discussing and thinking about strategic issues and challenges • Involve team members in scenario planning • Encourage team members to be active in reviewing the external context and to consider the nature of the internal context impacting the decision-making process • Encourage team members to suggest new ways of working and support them in implementing these • Encourage experimentation
Strategic perspective	• Work with the team to conduct stakeholder analyses when facing decisions or implementation of changes • Ask team members for proposals relating to key decisions and changes; ensure that they are briefed to consider both short- and long-term actions and implications
Managing resources	• Provide team members with an overall frame for actions and operations and give them the freedom to develop detailed implementation plans within the frame • Operate a 'by exception' approach to monitoring the delivery of actions; avoid overly intrusive levels of reporting • In reviewing projects and plans work with the team members to get their views on relative success and the learning that can be taken and applied to improve decision implementation
Achieving	• Involve team members in discussion of key goals and objectives for the organisation/your part of the organisation • Listen carefully to input and ideas from team members • Within the goals agreed as priorities, encourage team members to set personally aspirational objectives • Encourage team members to contribute to the prioritisation of actions and deployment of resources in a way that creates the greatest level of benefits

	CEO profile	Enabling
Personal Enablers		
Critical analysis and judgement	**High**	Medium
Vision and imagination	**High**	Medium
Strategic perspective	**High**	Medium
Managing resources	**High**	Low
Self-awareness	*Medium*	High
Emotional resilience	High	High
Intuitiveness	*Medium*	High
Interpersonal Enablers		
Interpersonal sensitivity	*Medium*	High
Influence	*Medium*	High
Engaging communication	*Medium*	High
Empowering	*Low*	High
Developing	*Medium*	High
Drivers		
Motivation	High	High
Achieving	**High**	Medium
Constrainer		
Conscientiousness	High	High

From this analysis it was evident that the CEO had a significant range of elements that needed to be addressed. He needed to reduce the impact of his high scores (shown in bold) and develop his lower scores (shown in italics). In discussing his profile and 'fit' in a coaching session he realised that he was acting in a very leader centric or 'heroic' manner.

From this case example we can see that the analysis of the individual profile against the 'best-fit' profile gives a clear indication of the overall development needs in order to build effective leadership capability. The needs can also be validated against how you as a leader are experiencing working with your team. This is illustrated further by the case study.

Case Example: Assessment (continued)
   In the course of the coaching discussion with the CEO the consequences of his leader-centric style were explored. In the course of this conversation the CEO realised that a consequence of his style was a failure to fully engage members of his executive team with the strategy and goals of the organisation. Furthermore, he realised that his view that the team lacked innovation was a direct conse-quence of his style. It also became apparent that the team members took their

cue from his style and behaved in a similar way with their direct reports. This was realised to be a significant cause of the low levels of employee engagement evidenced by the consistently low scores in the annual engagement survey.

Once development needs have been identified it is necessary to determine how they are going to be met. This takes us to the next step in the framework.

2.4   Step 4: Determining Development Priorities

In formulating a plan to develop emotionally intelligent leadership it is important to recognise that undertaking development requires time and effort. It is also important to recognise that attempting too much at once can lead to frustration and failure to realise the changes needed. Therefore, it is necessary to prioritise your effort and actions.

As we pointed out, in discussing the development of EI (see Chapter 5), some of the elements are easier to develop than others. In this context we introduced our 'vessel' metaphor. The same considerations apply to the overall leadership dimensions. Table 9.4 shows the relative ease of development across the 15 dimensions using the 'Develop to Exploit' scale.

Table 9.4   Development levels

Dimension	Develop	<------->	Exploit
Self-awareness	X		
Emotional resilience		X	
Motivation		X	
Sensitivity	X		
Influence	X		
Intuitiveness			X
Conscientiousness			X
Critical analysis and judgement			X
Vision and imagination		X	
Strategic perspective		X	
Engaging communication	X		
Managing resources	X		
Empowering	X		
Developing	X		
Achieving		X	

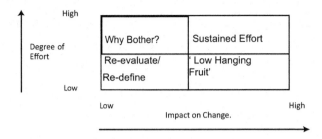

Fig. 9.2 Prioritisation framework

This provides one aspect that we need to consider when working on establishing development priorities. Clearly we are likely to get earlier results from development actions that relate to elements in the 'develop' column. Those in the middle column will be harder to develop and take longer. Those in the 'exploit' column will be the hardest to work on.

In thinking about the priorities for development there are a number of ways in which we can make choices about the priorities. One way of doing this is to consider the 'model' presented in Chapter 5. This is shown again in Fig. 9.2.

In using this framework, you should map your development needs onto the matrix. In essence, you should not have any needs on the left-hand side of the grid. If you do it may be that you have included elements in the profile analysis that do not need to change to get an optimum match to the required leadership style for the current or near future context. If you find this has happened, then re-examine your profile and check that you have not included any of these in your needs analysis. It is important to concentrate on the needs that fall into the right-hand side of the matrix. In general, it is important that you look at a mix of needs that include some short-term wins ('low-hanging fruit'). The reason for this is that achieving some early movement in your development will help in maintaining your effort and commitment to the changes that you want to achieve.

It is very helpful at this stage to discuss your plans with your team members to both check on your assumptions and/or make them aware of the development that you are planning to undertake. If you are working with a coach or mentor then you could also discuss priorities with him/her. In identifying priorities, it is important to achieve a balance between those needs that will have the greatest impact on changing your style, dealing with the largest profile gaps, and achieving some relatively early progress. However, you do need to be aware that developing any of the elements is not a quick process. Changing any element of the profile requires achieving a shift in both your mind-set and behaviours. It can take a few months to embed such changes. However, it is also worth noting that we have found that many of the elements are inter-correlated. This means that a shift in one element may well result in a related shift in another. For example, increasing your levels of interpersonal sensitivity may well have 'knock on' effects on both influence and engaging communication.

Prioritising should also take account of the development support and resources available to you. For example, if you have the facility to access a coach then achieving a shift in behaviour may be easier than having to rely purely on your own efforts. The prioritisation process may be illustrated further by returning to our case example.

Case Example: Prioritising Development
In the review of the CEO's profile and 'fit' analysis a large number of development needs were identified. In working with his coach the overarching theme for the changes needed related to engaging and involving his team. Working together they identified that a high-impact change would be to increase the empowering element significantly. However, this was recognised as being a change that would require sustained effort. The shorter term changes that would support this development would be to increase the levels of 'interpersonal sensitivity' and 'developing'. At the same time reducing the current levels of 'managing resources' would also contribute to the increase in the 'empowering' level. It was also seen to be likely that these changes could well lead to a positive shift in 'engaging communication' and 'influence'.

These priorities were then discussed with the team who welcomed them and were very supportive of the development plans.

Some four months after the start of the development actions the CEO undertook a 360° assessment, using the LDQ, and found notable shifts in the dimen-

sions that had been prioritised as well as in 'influence' and 'engaging communication'. This result motivated the CEO to then start to work on the more difficult areas of 'intuitiveness' and 'achieving'.

Whilst establishing priorities for development it is important to recognise that critical to success is your motivation to change. Before embarking on development it is important to establish clearly that you believe that these changes are important to the achievement of both your, and the organisation's goals.

2.5   Step 5: Plan Development Actions

Having identified your development needs and identified the priority dimensions to be developed it is necessary to think about actions that will enable these to be changed. Whilst some structured training interventions may be available to help with the development needs it is important to recognise that you are seeking behavioural change that can often involve a change in your mind-sets and beliefs about your current behaviours. Change requires action in practice—sustained effort to embed the new behaviours in your day-to-day practices as a leader.

A useful start point in planning development actions is to consider the following questions:

- What are the behaviours that I currently exhibit in relation to each of the dimensions I have identified for development?
- Why am I exhibiting these behaviours?
- How do I feel about my current behaviours?
- What do I see as the consequences of these behaviours?
- What are the barriers to change?
- What are the benefits to me of changing these behaviours?
- What are the benefits to the organisation of changing these behaviours?
- What will be the benefits to my team members of these behaviours?
- What will the new behaviours look like?
- How will I feel about behaving in a different way?

This process of reflection helps to uncover some important areas that will inform your development action plan. For example, if you feel that your focus on critical analysis and judgement in a transformational context is because you do not feel that your team members have the capability to exercise this capability, you might find it difficult to shift this assumption without actions to develop their capability and enabling them to practice and exercise their developed abilities. Alternatively, you may need to test your assumption: have you provided the opportunities for team members to display critical analysis and judgement? Going through this process will enable you to formulate clear development actions that will have a sustained impact.

Too often, in planning development, we forget to reflect on our strengths and consider how we can deploy them to support the development of the gaps in our repertoire as a leader. It is important to capture this reflection in a structured way as a basis for formulating a development action plan. Table 9.5 provides a possible framework that you might wish to use for this purpose.

Having undertaken this reflection process you are then ready to develop your action plan. In doing this you do need to consider how you will know that development is having the effect that you intended. An important aspect in assessing progress is to make use of feedback. As you are looking to develop leadership behaviours the most valuable source of feedback will be that provided by your team members. It is important to get feedback throughout the development process and you should include provision for feedback in your development plan. We have already raised the importance of feedback in Chapter 5 and it would be worth looking back over those comments when formulating your development plan.

In putting together the development plan you should be as specific as possible and set realistic timeframes. Although you may have identified a range of development needs, it makes sense to formulate your initial development plan to cover your initial priority needs. Table 9.6 outlines a format to consider using in creating your development plan.

Table 9.5 Development planning framework

Dimensions to develop	Current behaviours	Reasons for current behaviours	Benefits of change	Barriers to change	New behaviours	Feelings
	What are my current behaviours in this dimension?	Why am I using these behaviours?	What are the benefits: for me, my team, and the organisation, of changing behaviours?	What are the barriers to making the changes to my behaviours?	What will the new behaviours look like?	How will I feel when exhibiting the new behaviours?

Table 9.6 Format for development plan

Leadership dimension	Development need	Development goal	Actions planned	Support/resources needed	Feedback planned	Target dates
	What needs to change?	What is the end goal you are trying to achieve?	What are the specific actions that you plan to undertake?	What resources and support do you require?	How and how often will you be getting feedback?	When do you plan to implement and complete the actions?

Once you have completed the initial plan it is useful to take a careful look to establish how feasible it appears to be. If it seems too unrealistic you should revisit your priority assessment and see how the plan can be adapted to meet a smaller number of priority dimensions.

Once again, it is well worth discussing the plan with your team members. This can serve two purposes. Firstly, it will provide a way of communicating your intentions to the team and engaging them with your journey. Secondly, their feedback can provide a reality check in terms of scope and timescales. The process can be illustrated further by returning to our case example.

Case Example: Preparing the Development Plan

The CEO's development priorities were: reducing the impact of his 'managing resources dimension' and increasing the dimensions of 'interpersonal sensitivity' and 'developing'. In working through his planning reflections with his coach he realised that he had made a number of assumptions about his behaviours and about his team members. These were fed into the first step of his development planning. An extract from the reflection summary for the dimension of 'managing resources' is shown below.

Dimensions to develop	Current behaviours	Reasons for current behaviours	Benefits of change	Barriers to change	New behaviours	Feelings
Managing resources (reduce the impact)	Currently tend to do all of the planning for the team and organisation. Set goals for the team. Coordinate the performance of the team. Monitor performance and delivery regularly both in team meetings an individual weekly meetings.	I work in this way as the team do not seem to be particularly committed and do not seem to see the bigger picture. The lack of commitment of team members results in late delivery of work allocated and missed targets unless I keep their 'toes to the fire'. I am not sure that they are really as competent as I would expect.	Fewer demands on my time. More confidence in committing to goals with the board. Improved team performance	The capabilities of the team members. My own assumptions about the team members. My belief that I can do the job better than they can.	I will be setting a general frame for team members and give them more freedom to act. I will review progress less frequently and only at the heading level. I will involve the team in the annual and monthly planning processes	Nervous!! Ideally less stressed and able to enjoy other aspects of the role. Satisfied in seeing others grow.

The case example now moves on to the development action plan. The CEO used these reflections as the basis for formulating his action plan. An example of this for the same dimension (managing resources) is shown below.

Leadership dimension	Development need	Development goal	Actions planned	Support/resources needed	Feedback planned	Target dates
Managing resources	Reduce the impact of this dimension within the overall profile	Greater involvement of the team in planning and co-ordinating. Less direct monitoring and control of team planning and resourcing of work.	Discuss planned change at next team meeting to discuss next quarter's plans. Set frame for individual team members and overall team. Reduce individual review meetings from weekly to monthly. Focus reviews on high level issues rather than details.	Continued working with coach. Commitment and support from team members.	Feedback from team at each monthly meeting. Feedback from individual team members at regular individual meetings.	Start at next quarterly team meeting. Fully implemented within 6 months

The CEO discussed the overall plan for the initial development with his team and gained their commitment to work with him.

Once the development action plan has been finalised the next step is the implementation phase.

2.6   Step 6: Implementation and Review

The implementation of the plan should include a regular review of progress. The timing of the reviews will depend on the timescales within the plan. However, we would suggest that a review be conducted on a monthly basis. This review should include obtaining feedback from team members. The development plan should be seen as a living document. Changes may need to be made based on information and views that come to light during the review discussions.

At the end of the period of the initial plan it can be useful to conduct a final review. This final review should capture what has been learned about yourself and the process. This learning can prove to be helpful in terms of formulating further development plans.

It can be helpful to include in the final review a formal reassessment of the leadership dimensions and the context. A good way of doing this is to use the LDQ tool on a 360° basis. In this way you can see the effectiveness of the development actions and subsequently identify the next phase of development planning. This entails going through steps 2–6 again. Whilst this may seem a lot of effort, it will be very much quicker the second time around. In addition the benefits of the effort involved will be the development of a leadership profile that will lead to more effective leadership performance on a sustainable basis.

3   Conclusions

Throughout the book we have been emphasising the importance of developing a more engaging and facilitating style of leadership that is necessary for today's more complex and volatile environment. The approach we have outlined presents a way of moving towards such an approach by carefully linking the leadership dimensions to the context of the organisation. In this chapter we have outlined an approach to developing context relevant leadership that will lead to a more effective organisation. However, to date we have been focusing on the individual leader, even though we have suggested involving the team in the process. Increasingly we are finding that leadership is not a solo activity and the function is increasingly shared within a team. In the next chapter we will explore the development of emotionally intelligent leadership teams.

Notes

1. See *The Leadership Dimensions Questionnaire Manual*, published by VDA Assessment & Development Consultants, for a full range of references that underpin the LDQ model and related assessment tools.
2. The LDQ is an assessment tool that is developed from the authors' work. It is published by VDA Assessment & Development Consultants.
3. The LDQ Self is published by VDA Assessment & Development Consultants. A 360° version is also available.

10

Emotionally Intelligent Leadership Teams

1   Introduction

We have been considering the increasing significance of a more engaging and facilitating style of leadership in organisations as they face increasingly complex and volatile contexts. In doing this we have suggested that EI is becoming an increasingly important aspect of leadership in some contexts. We have then expanded this into the model of emotionally intelligent leadership that combines EQ with cognitive and managerial competencies (the LDQ model).

In looking at the nature of Emotionally Intelligent leadership we have identified that EQ can be developed (Chapter 5) and this also applies to the broader LDQ model (Chapters 8 and 9). To date we have focused on these concepts at the individual level. However, as organisations have developed to deal with rapidly changing contexts we have seen the emergence of an increasing focus on the role and effectiveness of team-based approaches to deliver effective performance and cope with the challenges of implementing change on a regular, even continuous, basis. Therefore, in this chapter we will move from considering individual leaders to exploring the development of emotionally intelligent leadership teams.

© The Editor(s) (if applicable) and the Author(s) 2016
M. Higgs, V. Dulewicz, *Leading with Emotional Intelligence*,
DOI 10.1007/978-3-319-32637-5_10

2   The Growth in Importance of Teams

2.1   Drivers of Interest in Teams and Team Working

There has no doubt been an increasing focus on teams and team working within organisations—both in terms of research and practice. This is not just a fad, but rather is a response to a number of drivers that lead to a need to work differently. These are:

- *Changes in organisational structures*

We have seen increasing complexity in the organisational environment and context. As organisations have responded to changing contexts we have seen the emergence of a move to structures that are flatter. There has been a notable reduction in the number of levels of management and with those in them and thus managerial leadership roles have increasing spans of control. In responding to this there has been a recognition that this requires a move to manage in different ways in order to deal with the complexities that arise in flatter organisations.

- *Increasing importance of innovation as a response to volatile and radically changing contexts*

As the environment in which organisations operate becomes more uncertain, complex and volatile there is a need to find new ways of working and competing. This gives rise to a need to encourage innovation in all aspects of an organisation's work. Research has shown that team-based working is one way of creating a climate that encourages higher levels of innovation.

- *Dealing with the challenges of change*

As we discussed in Chapter 7 one of the major challenges faced by organisations is to be able to implement change successfully. The rate of change, resulting from the volatile, ambiguous and complex environment, is increasing. Research has shown that working through teams is one way of increasing the likelihood of change being successfully implemented (Higgs & Rowland, 2005). In addition, research has also shown that teams are very effective in dealing with complex issues and challenges (Higgs, 2007).

* *Changing views of the nature of leadership*

In Chapter 6 we discussed the developments in thinking about the nature of leadership required in today's context. In particular the development of thinking in terms of distributed and shared leadership points to the need to place a greater emphasis on team working.

* *Increasing pressures for organisations to perform*

One of the consequences of the contexts in which organisations find themselves today is that there are growing pressures to deliver ever improving levels of performance. In the private sector this is seen in terms of increasing demands for the delivery of shareholder value. In the public sector there is a constant demand for providing value for money services and reducing costs. Research has shown that effective team working has a significant impact on performance. This seems to be a particularly notable finding in relation to senior and top management teams. Given these drivers it is evident that we need to place a greater emphasis on understanding how teams work and what makes an effective team.

3   Research on Teams

There has probably been more research conducted by occupational psychologists into groups than into any other topic, with the possible exception of leadership. Most of this has identified two totally independent dimensions of group work—those activities related to the task and its achievement; and those related to the interpersonal relationships (the people aspects) sometimes referred to as 'process' factors. A semantic complication has been the interchangeability of the words group and team, without any clear definition given. In our view, a *team* is a group, but with the following additional characteristics:

- all members share common aims,
- all members share responsibility for outcomes,
- all members are highly committed to achieving common objectives and high-quality results,
- the members are interdependent, and
- individual success equates to group success.

Overall when looking at a team the whole is greater than the sum of the parts.

The contribution of effective teamworking, particularly amongst top teams, is an enduring topic within management literature. In the popular literature there appears to be a common assumption that the case for teamworking is proven and well understood. In their book *The wisdom of teams* Katzenbach and Smith (1993) make two statements which typify the assumptions frequently adopted:

1. *It is obvious that teams outperform individuals.*
2. *Team is a word and concept well known to everyone.*

However, even a cursory review of the vast literature on teams and teamworking reveals that these assumptions are, at the best, questionable. The importance, ascribed by organisations and authors, to teams and teamworking necessitates the provision of rigorous evidence to support such assertions. Whilst much of the evidence presented to support the value of teams does tend to be derivative from group research, there has been more recent direct, team-based, empirical work that provides evidence that teams do lead to higher levels of performance, innovation and building of climates that increase levels of employee engagement. Indeed much of the more recent research has focused on the impact of leadership and senior management teams on the performance and development of organisations. The links demonstrated between organisational performance and top team characteristics and embedded in what has been termed 'Upper Echelon Theory' (Hambrick & Mason, 1984).

The most celebrated work on management teams was conducted by Dr Meredith Belbin, Aston, and Mottram (1976) over a ten-year period at Henley Management College. They studied literally hundreds of syndicates (teams) working on a business simulation exercise in which they ran their companies over a simulated three-year period, all competing with similar products in the same market. Not only did the researchers have the results of the business performance of each team; they also had personality profiles and mental-ability test results, and detailed behavioural records of how each member of each team had actually performed throughout the week-long exercise. After thorough analysis of the composition and behaviour of both high- and low-performing teams a number of 'team roles' were identified. These constitute clusters of related behaviours that some managers demonstrated by dint of their personality and intellectual ability. The team roles covered not only the task and people dimensions, but added a third: ideas. In other words, a 'team role' is a preference or predisposition to behave in a certain way over a period of time. Eight different team roles were identified by Belbin and colleagues:

- *Plant*: The creative, ideas person.
- *Resource investigator*: The networker and entrepreneur.
- *Co-ordinator*: The participative leader.
- *Shaper*: The driving, up-front leader.
- *Monitor evaluator*: The intelligent, analytical critic.
- *Team worker*: The people-oriented facilitator.
- *Implementer*: The task implementation person.
- *Completer finisher*: The quality-assurer and time-keeper.

More detailed descriptions of each role's positive characteristics and personality factors, and allowable weaknesses, are presented in Table 10.1.

Belbin's original work, and many other research and case-studies conducted subsequently, have shown that management teams in which all eight roles are filled by at least one person perform at a much higher level, in a wider range of different tasks, than other less well 'balanced' teams. An important caveat is that there should, ideally, not be more than one shaper, and not too many plants in a team, otherwise there is

Table 10.1 Team role definitions and related personality descriptors

Roles and descriptions team role contributions	Allowable weaknesses	Personality factors	
Plant (PL): Creative, imaginative, unorthodox. Solves difficult problems.	Weak in communication with and managing ordinary people.	Assertive Venturesome Detached Forthright Serious	Experimenting Tender-minded Intelligent Imaginative Self-sufficient Radical
Resource investigator (RI): Extravert, enthusiastic, communicative. Explores opportunities. Develops contacts.	Loses interest once initial enthusiasm has passed.	Calm Venturesome Imaginative	Trusting
Co-ordinator (CO): Mature, confident and trusting. A good chairman. Clarifies goals, promotes decision-making.	Not necessarily the most clever or creative member of a group.	Calm Assertive Trusting Enthusiastic	Detached Practical Conscientious Controlled
Shaper (SH): Dynamic, outgoing, highly strung. Challenges, pressurises, finds way round obstacles.	Prone to provocation and short-lived bursts of temper.	Tense Anxious Assertive Venturesome	Expedient Tough-minded Suspicious Apprehensive
Monitor evaluator (ME): Sober, strategic and discerning. Sees all options. Judges accurately	Lacks drive and ability to inspire others.	Intelligent Serious-minded	Shrewd
Team worker (TW): Social, mild, perceptive and accommodating. Listens, builds, averts friction.	Indecisive in crunch situations.	Outgoing Trusting	Unassertive Group-oriented
Implementer (IM): Disciplined, reliable, conservative and efficient. Turns ideas into practical actions.	Somewhat inflexible, slow to respond to new possibilities.	Conscientious Tough-minded Practical	Trusting Conservative Controlled
Completer finisher (CF): Painstaking, conscientious, anxious. Searches out errors and omissions. Delivers on time.	Inclined to worry unduly. Reluctant to delegate.	Anxious Tense Controlled	Conscientious Apprehensive

likely to be friction and division in the former case, and too much talking and not enough action in the latter. Belbin's 'theory' is now extremely well established, and widely used around the world. It has also been copied by many other management academics and consultants, endorsing the recognition of its usefulness. Whilst Belbin's original work related to senior management teams it has subsequently been shown that the theory 'works' with junior management and non-management teams. A key word in describing the theory is '*balance*'. A team of different individuals, each with a distinctive set of strengths and allowable weaknesses, is likely to perform better than a team of, for example, highly bright and dynamic 'superstars', all of whom are from the same mould.

4   Emotional Intelligence and Teams

As EI has grown in its acceptance in both research and practice there has been an increasing interest in the concept of team EI. However, in spite of interest in the idea, to date, there has been little success in developing a team level measure of EI. Perhaps this is unsurprising as EI is clearly an individual level concept. This is not to say that there is no value in looking at the concept of EI within a team. Indeed we would suggest that it is important to do so. We have found that EI in teams is best explored by examining the way in which individuals within the team differ in terms of their strengths and weaknesses in terms of the different elements of their EI. This can be done by exploring the way in which individual elements are in balance within the team.

'Balance' is emphasised in understanding the performance of teams. It is also a critical feature of our model of EI, described in Chapter 3. So, are there common principles between Belbin's theory of teams and our model of EI that can be used to build better teams? We believe there are, and the results from our own study of managers (see Chapter 4) provided us with some pointers. Since we had personality profiles for our entire sample, we were able to calculate each person's team roles. Several distinct similarities emerged between specific Belbin Team Roles (TRs) and the elements of EI, within the framework of our model, with its three main features.

4.1   Drivers

Two TRs seemed to fit neatly into this category. Those with *high* EI motivation are likely to play the *shaper* role, and to drive the team to achieving goals, and ultimately to success. In addition, the *resource investigator*, being highly energetic and enthusiastic, is usually very effective at motivating fellow team members, and spotting opportunities for the team to exploit. (The *resource investigator* also probably fits under the enablers.)

4.2   Constrainers

One TR has links with these EI characteristics. The *completer finisher*, being a perfectionist, the person preoccupied with quality and timing, is likely to possess the EI qualities of conscientiousness, and will therefore apply these characteristics to good effect. He or she will probably curb the excesses of expedient colleagues and demand high standards of output from colleagues, and will probably bring the team back on track whenever it is behind time. Much time can be saved by exposing and rejecting flawed ideas at an early stage.

4.3   Intrapersonal and Interpersonal Enablers

The enablers embrace not only the EI elements of influence, self-awareness and sensitivity, but also IQ and MQ. Those with high influence, self-awareness and sensitivity, and with high MQ, especially appraising and developing staff and communication, are probably fitted to play the *co-ordinator* role very effectively, in terms of leading the team in a democratic, participative, 'hands-off' style. In contrast, those with just the three EI elements are likely to be well fitted to the purely people-focused *team worker* role, the person who will concentrate on building group cohesion, encourage communications between members and reduce conflict and disharmony. Those who are highly conscientious and practical are the ones who would make good *implementers*, those who have a 'hands-on' role in implementing any action plans designed by colleagues. Those individuals who score highly on EI intuitiveness, and who also have high

IQ, are probably suited to the monitor evaluator role. Finally, the sensitive members with high IQ and a creative streak are the ones who would most probably play the *plant* role, the member who generates most of the creative ideas and proposals.

We have already mentioned that those who are highly enthusiastic and who in turn motivate colleagues have many of the *resource investigator* characteristics. This role however could also be seen as an 'enabling' role, especially for those individuals who score highly on EQ influence (good for networking and exploiting opportunities) and who also have high MQ, in particular good communication skills and business sense. These are the team members who will create business opportunities and win new customers for the team. The expansion of the development of emotionally intelligent leadership teams using the core view that:

Emotionally Intelligent Leadership $= EQ + IQ + MQ$ will be explored further in this chapter.

A summary of the links between EI elements and team roles is presented in Fig. 10.1. This demonstrates the potential for using the EI model on a team basis, for bringing together individuals whose own EI scores may not be in balance, but who nevertheless collectively complement each other's' strengths and allowable weaknesses, to improve team cohesion and performance.

We can all think of teams who perform badly because they are not well balanced, and because members do not complement each other. There are many football or cricket teams that spring to mind, but let us take a look at two examples of dysfunctional work teams where EI is out of balance. First, consider a sales team, with members all from the same mould. They all score highly on the enablers—they are very persuasive and good at influencing other people; and they are responsive and sensitive to the needs and feelings of other people. They are also very high on motivation—they are enthusiastic, dynamic, energetic individuals, who are all driven to succeed and to attain high targets. To do so they are very decisive people, who make decisions on the spur of the moment, based upon their intuition and 'gut-feel'. In contrast, however, they have a low level of awareness of their own feelings and emotions, and are unable to handle them effectively. Importantly, they are not very conscientious and have a low level of integrity. What are the consequences of this unbalanced

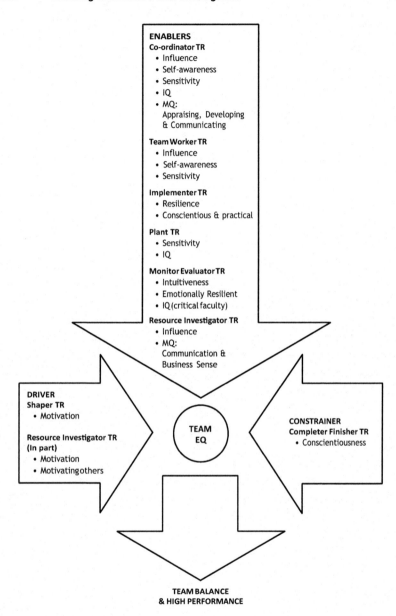

Fig. 10.1   Team EQ and team roles

EI team likely to be? It will most probably produce a very exhilarating and enjoyable atmosphere, with a lot of energy and enthusiasm demonstrated, and a constant buzz of excitement and expectation. Individuals are likely to create a highly sociable atmosphere, with an emphasis not only on achieving targets but also on having fun. However, because none of the team members are high on the EI constrainers, everyone is likely to cut corners and to show a lack of concern about meeting deadlines, or about the quality of the service or product being offered. All of them are likely to bend, if not break the rules if it helps to achieve results, and some may even transgress the law. When performance falls or problems occur, as they inevitably will, with low resilience there will come friction and disharmony within the team caused by an inability of all members to control their feelings and disappointments. More often than not, this results in a downward spiral of performance, which is very difficult to arrest.

Another type of dysfunctional team is one in which many or all members have high enablers but, in contrast to the first team, motivation is low and the conscientiousness of all members is very high. This team is preoccupied with the detail and with getting everything just right. Everything has to be done by the book. There will also be a preoccupation with the quality of the output, even if it takes three times as long to achieve that final 5 % of quality. Members lack intuitiveness and spend forever seeking more and more information before being willing to take a decision. They also lack energy and motivation, and sometimes run out of steam before they complete the task. With a lack of urgency and purpose things are readily put off until tomorrow. In such a team there is also a predisposition to concentrate on the short-term tasks and to forget about the long-term objectives or final output. The atmosphere is unlikely to be stimulating or exciting, and there is likely to be a preoccupation with one's own feelings, and the feelings of other members. This in turn can lead to a preoccupation with how the team is working and why the members are not feeling fulfilled, to the detriment of task achievement, the ultimate purpose of a work team. We can all think of times when we have been on the receiving end of such teams.

So what would constitute a high performing EI team? First, not everyone has to have high scores on all seven elements of EI. A fairly balanced set of scores within an individual's profile would be desirable—it would be unrealistic to expect that all members of a team had high scores on all elements, plus high IO and MQ. Indeed, a team of superstars would probably not work well together and would demonstrate conflict and disharmony. The requirements for a successful EI team are:

- at least one or two members who have very high motivation;
- one or two members who are conscientious and who possess high levels of conscientiousness and integrity; and
- most, if not all, members who have average or above scores on the enablers—self-awareness, resilience, influence, intuitiveness and interpersonal sensitivity.

It would also be beneficial for the team to contain at least one or two members with high IQ and high MQ—the management competencies of business sense, communication skills and staff-management skills.

In such a team the drivers would be kept in check by those who were conscientious and who had high ethical standards. Some would concentrate on producing and evaluating ideas. Some would focus on influencing people and getting new business and achieving results and others could focus on organisation and team working. There would be a positive and exciting atmosphere, in which debate and argument would thrive, but would be handled maturely and productively. Members would gravitate to those tasks that fitted their preferences and abilities, and the whole would be more than the sum of its parts—the essence of effective team work.

Team development, using the EI model, requires two main components:

1. working on the development of the EI of individual team members; and
2. exploring the relative strengths and weaknesses of the individual members and developing ways of working that make the most of the capabilities of the whole team.

In those instances where it is not possible for management to conduct a TR analysis on their staff because the psychometric personality data are not available, our research to date suggests that it could well be advantageous to analyse the EI profiles of each member, in order to explore the overall EI balance of the team, in terms of drivers, constrainers and enablers. As with the Belbin analysis, if the team is deficient in certain areas, and since we believe that EI elements can be developed or exploited, special development action should be considered in cases where individuals currently have an average score. If, however, there are gaps which no one in the team is likely to be able to fill, even with development, then this suggests that management might have to revert to the 'transfer market', to bring in new talent.

5   Developing the Leadership Team

As discussed above, there is a growth in the importance of developing effective senior leadership teams. Their performance as a team is found to have a significant impact on the performance of the organisation. In considering the relationship of EI to TR and the balance within a team we have already indicated that EI needs to be considered alongside the IQ of the team members and their MQ. This is particularly important when we consider the performance and development of leadership teams. Indeed the context in which such teams need to operate requires consideration of the overall model of emotionally intelligent leadership that we presented in Chapter 8.

In Belbin's work on team performance and balance he pointed out that an effective team needs to achieve a balance between roles that focus on ideas, tasks and people. Whilst his TR model can be presented in these terms, there is scope for extending this by considering the components of our model of EQ + IQ + MQ. Table 10.2 below provides a summary of how the components of the Emotionally Intelligent Leadership can be mapped onto the ideas, task and people balance.

In using this framework for the development of an emotionally intelligent leadership team there are a number of steps involved:

1. *Assess individual members of the team against the LDQ elements.* Ideally this assessment should be carried out using the Leadership Dimensions Questionnaire (LDQ).[1] This will produce the individual profiles that

Table 10.2 Team roles and LDQ

Balance components	Team roles	LDQ elements
Ideas	Plant	Critical analysis (IQ)
	Monitor evaluator	Vision and imagination (IQ)
		Intuitiveness (EQ)
Task	Shaper	Managing resources (MQ)
	Implementer	Conscientiousness (EQ)
	Completer finisher	Motivation (EQ)
		Achieving (MQ)
People	Co-ordinator	Interpersonal sensitivity (EQ)
	Resource investigator	Influence (EQ)
	Team worker	Communication (MQ)
		Empowerment (EQ)
		Developing (MQ)
		Perspective (IQ)

should be used to develop each team member's capabilities against the context in which they are working (as discussed in Chapter 8).

2. *Produce a summary analysis of the total team.* This entails presenting the average score on each element as well as identifying the highest and lowest scores in the teams. The analysis should also include a summary of the team's potential strengths and weaknesses based on the average profile. Fig. 10.2 shows an example team profile.

3. *Conduct a team workshop to review and discuss the profile.* This workshop is important for a number of reasons. Firstly, the team should agree on the context level in which they are operating (i.e., the degree of change being faced). This, in turn helps to establish the style that is appropriate for the context (see Chapter 8). Secondly, the team can review and agree their strengths and weaknesses as a team. In doing this it is helpful to consider other sources of data that may validate the analysis (e.g., data from staff engagement surveys, problems in delivering projects, delays in implementing plans). Ideally the team will also share their individual profiles. This will enable a more detailed discussion of areas that can be addressed as a team. Finally, the team can agree on actions that they will take as a team to address the weaknesses they have identified. These actions can either relate to changing how they work with each other (based on understanding more about each other) or how they will allocate tasks based on the strengths of individuals.

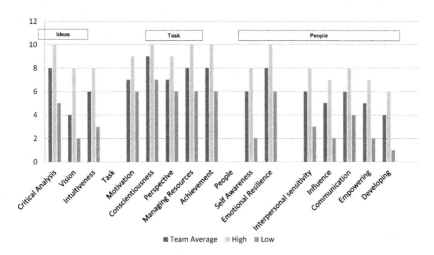

Fig. 10.2 Team profile

4. *Implement and review action plans agreed.* In implementing actions it is important that progress is reviewed regularly. As actions are likely to involve behaviour change it is important to ensure that feedback is obtained. If changes involve different behaviours during team meetings then each meeting should include a process review. Broader actions will entail getting feedback from others in the organisation.

In focusing on the team it is important that individual development actions are not forgotten. The ideal situation will clearly be reached when all team members have fully developed their capabilities to the level needed to match the context in which they are working. The application of this framework is illustrated further in the case study below.

6   Case Example

Advizors is an international professional services company that operates in over 20 countries. It is a long-established firm that offers consulting services across a wide range of sectors. It grew significantly between the 1990s and early 2000s. It then maintained a strong market position until

2012. Since then it has faced rapidly growing competition from both new entrants to the market and established competitors.

Advizors has operated based on running a range of specialised consulting practices that each operate relatively autonomously. However, they have recognised that clients are increasingly looking for integrated solutions that meet their needs. The executive team of Advizors have identified that the organisation will need to move to working with clients by bringing together multidisciplinary teams. This will mean working in a very different way and developing the capability of the organisation to introduce effective team working. They decided that the top leadership team should set an example to the organisation and be the first team to undertake a team-development programme.

The top team comprises the CEO, the senior directors of the four main operating practices, the finance director, the COO and the HR director. The starting point of their development programme was to undertake individual assessments using the LDQ. The profile of the team, using the Belbin related analysis of the LDQ elements (Ideas, Task and People), is shown in Fig. 10.2. From this analysis the team spent some time discussing their potential strengths and weaknesses as a team. These are summarised in Table 10.3 below.

The team agreed with this analysis. They felt that it was supported by evidence from the organisation. In particular, they found endorsement from the following:

- Low scores on the employee engagement survey;
- Delays in the implementation of projects;

Table 10.3 Team analysis

Potential strengths	Potential weaknesses
• Clear task focus	• Lack of innovation and creative thinking
• Drive to achieve and deliver	• Under-utilisation of people's potential
• Deadline conscious	• Low levels of engagement with strategy
• Quality of analysis	• Lack of attention to people issues
• External focus	• Close down on new ideas too early
• Strategic perspective	• Over-focus on goals and tasks
	• Need for complete data slows decision making

- Delays in approving or reaching decisions on business cases and other proposals presented to the team; and
- Increasing levels of unwanted attrition of junior- and middle-level consulting staff.

The view was that the major need to address the people issues identified and that it should be a priority. The team member with the strongest profile in relation to the people component of the profile was the Director of Advisors' strategy practice. The team agreed that she would be their champion in relation to the implementation of the integrated offering strategy and related move to team-based working.

They also recognised that, as a team, they needed to be more innovative and creative and to be more open to new ideas. They felt that one way of addressing this would be for the team to use a brainstorming technique when exploring new issues, challenges or ideas as well as when working on elements of business strategy. The COO was the strongest member of the team on vision and imagination and, therefore, they agreed that he would take the lead in brainstorming sessions.

The team then moved to explore the leadership profiles based on the LDQ in order to identify other actions that they may need to think about in order to become an emotionally intelligent leadership team. The full team profile is shown in Fig. 10.3.

As discussed in Chapter 9 an important starting point for any development discussion is to consider the leadership context. The individual team members had seen the context as either one of significant change or of transformational change. Given these different views the team discussed the context. In doing this it became evident that the changes in approach being implemented in the new strategy entailed a basic shift in the way in which the organisation needed to work and a fundamental shift in its core business model. Given this they felt that they really were facing a *transformational context*. Having agreed this then the team reviewed the profile that is indicated for an *engaging* leadership style (see Chapter 8/ Fig. 8.3). The team profile was then examined against the required engaging profile. In doing this they identified where, as a team, they needed to develop elements or moderate elements where they were overly strong as

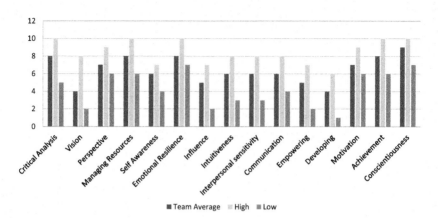

Fig. 10.3   Case of team LDQ

Table 10.4   Need for changes to the team LDQ profile

More focus	Less focus	Match
• Vision and imagination • Self-awareness • Interpersonal sensitivity • Influence • Intuitiveness • Engaging communication • Empowering • Developing	• Critical analysis • Strategic perspective • Managing resources • Achieving	• Emotional resilience • Motivation • Conscientiousness

well as elements where they clearly matched the profile. The results of this discussion are shown in Table 10.4.

This analysis reinforced the need for the team to move towards a greater people focus. In the course of the discussion the team realised that their individual profiles and the team profile were very much in the 'heroic' leader centric mode. The context was seen to be one of volatility, uncertainty, complexity and ambiguity, thus requiring a more engaging and facilitating approach. They identified a clear need for greater levels of empowerment and to ensure that people are engaged with the new strategy. They agreed, as a first step, to set up a two-day off-site meeting for the team and the extended leadership team (the direct reports of the executive team) to review the strategy and work on the details of its implementation. As a part of this they established that members of the extended team would become champions of the change relating to the business operations and to work with them to devolve more accountability for implementation. They also charged the HR Director with designing a development plan for all consulting staff, team leaders and managers.

As a team they agreed to focus on building employee engagement and all agreed to host meetings with staff to explore the issues raised by the last employee engagement survey. In addition to the team actions all members of the team undertook to work on their individual development needs. To this end coaches were engaged to work on an individual basis to facilitate the development of each team member. The team then introduced the LDQ assessment for all who were in leadership roles and again supported this with access to coaches.

The team also identified a need to ensure that the changes in their working should become embedded in their practice. They decided to ensure that all team meetings included a process review, examining both how they were working together and progressing with the planned actions, at the end of each meeting. Furthermore, they planned a rerun of the LDQ assessment at the end of 12 months as a measure of change. In order to work further on embedding the changes they instituted a 360° feedback process for themselves as a start before introducing it for all in leadership roles.

In a review of the impact of the changes after some 18 months they were able to identify that:

- The new strategy had been implemented successfully and had been welcomed by many of their clients.
- Revenues from consulting projects had increased by 18 % and a significant number of new clients had been attracted.
- Employee engagement scores had increased in each of the 6 monthly surveys over the period.
- Turnover of junior- and middle-level consultants had decreased.

Whilst no team member claimed that all outcomes were totally explained by the team assessment and development process the team were in no doubt that it had played an important role in achieving the outcomes. They were particularly buoyed by a comment from one of their direct reports who said:

I don't know how it happened, but the culture around here has been transformed—this is a much happier place to work in

However, the process was not without some pain. One of the consulting practice directors (a high-performing member of the team) was not convinced of the need for the changes, and left the organisation.

7   Conclusions

In exploring leadership, we have been arguing that in today's uncertain, volatile, complex and ambiguous context we need to move away from the traditional 'heroic' models of leadership. We have looked in earlier chapters at the implications of this and alternative more engaging and facilitating styles at the level of individual leaders. We have also emphasised the emergence of concepts of distributed and shared leadership. A particular focus of this development is the need to look at leadership at a team as well as at an individual level. The research into teams has increasingly highlighted the important role of leadership teams. In this chapter, we have explored this in the context of team research that emphasises balance and the work on EI at the team level.

We noted in Chapter 4 that the EI elements reflect a wide range of personality characteristics covering four of the five main dimensions of adult personality. In this chapter we have extended the EI model, from the individual to the group level of analysis, and have commented on the similarities between EI and Belbin's TR. We have also suggested that there is scope for using EI assessments to help in building balanced, and therefore effective and flexible teams. Based on the argument that:

Emotionally Intelligent Leadership $= EQ + IQ + MQ$

we have extended the balance to the whole range of elements that comprise our emotionally intelligent leadership model and suggested a framework for developing emotionally intelligent leadership teams. Working on developing such teams can (as illustrated by the case study) lead to a change in the culture of an organisation. Indeed, we might consider the work at the leadership team level contributes to the formation of an emotionally intelligent culture. In the next chapter we explore this idea further by looking at EI and the total organisation, and in particular how the organisation's culture affects the EI of individuals and teams working within it.

Note

1. The LDQ is published by VDA Assessment & Development Consultants.

Bibliography

Belbin, R. M., Aston, B. R., & Mottram, R. D. (1976). Building effective management teams. *Journal of General Management, 3*(3), 23–29.

Hambrick, D. C., & Mason, P. A. (1984). Upper echelons: The organisation as a reflection of its top managers. *Academy of Management Review, 9*, 193–206.

Higgs, M. J. (2007). What makes for top team success? A study to identify factors associated with successful performance of senior management teams. *Irish Journal of Management, 27*(2), 161–188.

Higgs, M. J., & Rowland, D. (2005). All changes great and small: Exploring approaches to change and its leadership. *Change Management Journal, 5*(2), 121–151.

Katzenbach, J. R., & Smith, D. K. (1993). *The wisdom of teams.* Boston, MA: Harvard Business School Press.

11

Emotionally Intelligent Leadership and Organisations

1   Introduction

So far, we have been examining the way in which our thinking about leadership has been developing as organisations face increasingly uncertain, volatile, complex and ambiguous contexts. We have explored the way in which effective leadership requires a move from the 'traditional' heroic model to one that is more engaging and facilitating. In doing this we have seen the growing significance of EI and the evolution of the need for emotionally intelligent leadership. In the previous chapter we examined the role that leadership teams can play in developing the performance of an organisation. In doing this we saw how the style and behaviours of the leadership team can impact the culture of the organisation and how, in particular, an emotionally intelligent leadership team can have a very positive effect on the engagement of employees in the organisation. The 'heroic' model of leadership is based on the view that it is the leader who delivers performance. However, in today's context this assumption is challenged. Higgs (2009) points out that this link between the leader and performance is not a direct one. He suggests that leaders

© The Editor(s) (if applicable) and the Author(s) 2016
M. Higgs, V. Dulewicz, *Leading with Emotional Intelligence*,
DOI 10.1007/978-3-319-32637-5_11

create a culture that enables the performance of the organisation (or possibly constrains it!).

In this chapter we explore the nature of organisational culture and how the determiners of culture are changing towards the development of the concept of an *emotionally intelligent culture*. We suggest that such a move can lead to more effective and sustainable organisational performance in the current context and environment.

2   Thinking about Organisations

In considering the area of organisation culture we need to consider our basic thinking about the nature of organisations. For much of the twentieth century the predominant thinking about organisations was influenced by the sociologist Max Weber[1] who proposed the idea of practical rationality that encompassed:

- Rational technique: the calculated use of means.
- Technical rationality: the progress from *technique* to the use of more effective means.
- Rational choice of ends (on the basis of *knowledge* and precise calculation).
- Life-guiding principles: action guided by *generalised* value principles.
- Rational-methodology lifestyle: the unification *and* balance of the above points to ensure their joint success.

He highlighted these points as a counterbalance to 'emotionality' that he saw as an integral and significant aspect of behaviour in an organisational context. Thus, he saw bureaucracy as a route to organisational control and a means of legitimising authority. Weber is often portrayed as the 'father' of rationality. However, he was far from disinterested in the 'emotional' aspects of organisations and was particularly interested in affectivity as one of his four types of social actions. It is stated frequently that Weber discounted emotions within his bureaucratic model of organisations. However, he did allow for emotion with bureaucracy, albeit that their rational understanding should become an intrinsic part of their working. Indeed, his work was designed to explore the dialectic between rationality and affectivity. To simplify the Weberian 'philosophy' the emphasis on rationality is concerned with rationalisation of both the instrumental and emotional aspects of organisation behaviour.

The translation of Weberian principles into managerial frameworks was epitomised by Taylor and his views on scientific management. This highly rational model provided the foundation of the production line approach to processes that influenced both practitioners and writers on management well into the 1950s. Arguably, the inheritance of this thinking has been seen in the way in which organisations worked well into the 1970s. It was perhaps not until the Total Quality Movement (TQM) became significant that the fundamental principles of Taylorism were challenged.

In this obsession with rationality in organisation and process design, the historical origins of Weber's work have been observed. Weber's call for rationality was underpinned by earlier concerns about the abuse of collective power voiced by influential writers in the period of the industrial revolution. Thus, the purpose (i.e., prevention of abuse of power) has been eclipsed by the process (i.e., the focus on bureaucracy as a means of ensuring rationality).

This focus reinforces Weber's nightmare of the 'disenchantment of the world'. This, fundamental point has been resurrected in the field of sociology by writers such as Albrow (1997). In a recent book he presented a collection of papers that addressed the topic of emotion in organisations and highlighted the importance of working with both the rational and emotional elements of behaviour in an organisational context.

While these developments have been taking place in the sociological arena, parallel developments have been taking place in the field of management and organisational behaviour. In the more popular and pragmatic world of business we have seen, in the last five years or so, a focus on 'people as a competitive advantage' and associated views and models relating to how we might develop and exploit this 'resource'. A stream of writing has been associated with this trend that has begun to examine the way in which emotion has been a neglected area when building approaches to developing managers and leaders. This growing emergence of thinking has tended to lead to a fundamental challenge to the

Cartesian conception of rationality that has dominated our education and opened our minds to new paradigms.

To a large extent the challenges faced by organisations in operating in an uncertain, complex, highly volatile, competitive and global environment have been shown to be inadequately addressed by the 'rational model' (and its many adaptations). This failure of the established ways of thinking about organisations has led to a growing focus on the non-rational aspects of organisation behaviour such as vision, mission and values, rather than the traditional rational focus on strategy, goals and objectives. Indeed the approaches to core strategy formulation have shifted from an exclusively analytical approach to the more intuitive and 'emotive' approach in the resource-based view of strategy. The links between such a shift in thinking and organisational success were highlighted in the book, *Built to Last*, by Collins and Porras (2005). In their book, they pointed to many drivers of corporate success that can be seen as being more readily associated with the 'emotional' than the 'rational' elements of the organisation. Typical of such claims are that the evidence demonstrates that the consistently successful organisations have a 'purpose beyond profit' and set 'Big, Hairy, Audacious Goals' (BHAGs). This is not the language of the analytical strategists and corporate planners. Yet it has clearly resonated with the practical experience of many leaders and is seen as offering a viable and, potentially more exciting, alternative to the failed volumes of strategy documents that seem incapable of implementation. The number of organisational executives who readily converse in terms of purpose, vision and even BHAGs is a testament to this shift in thinking. However, it is evident that organisational success does not result from the 'emotional' route alone (any more than, in reality, it did from the 'rational' route alone). The key to success appears to lie in achieving a balance between the emotional and rational strands of organisational thinking and behaviour. This need for balance is summarised in Fig. 11.1. Reviewing Fig. 11.1 illustrates that strategy has two components that lead down different implementation routes. Most leading thinkers and writers on strategy emphasise that implementation is critical to success. With the 'new' model it is clear that organisations need to be focused on both

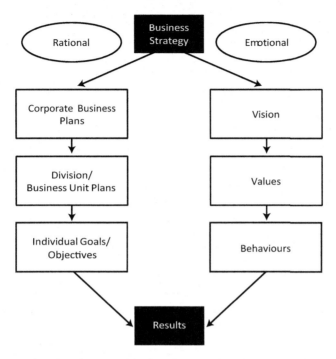

Fig. 11.1 Balancing the emotional and rational aspects

achieving results and aligning individual behaviours with their goals and strategy.

2.1   Relationship to Emotional Intelligence

Reviewing the arguments developed above will give rise to a recognition that there are clear parallels between these, at an organisational level, and the arguments for the significance of EI outlined in the earlier chapters of this book. Indeed much of the enthusiasm with which organisations have greeted the concept of EI may be seen to be a result of the new thinking in terms of drivers of corporate success. However, the very enthusiasm with which EI has been greeted in so many settings may be seen as its ability to explain individual performance and contribution—vital to corporate success, but evidently in short supply! Reflecting on the above leads us to raise two distinct, but related, questions:

- How do organisations encourage or develop the EI of their people?
- Can organisations be emotionally intelligent?

The first of these questions may be seen as being related to the extent to which the culture of the organisation recognises nurtures and promotes (in the broadest as well as specific sense) individuals who display elements of EI. Conversely, do some organisational cultures destroy or punish the exhibition of elements of EI by its people? The second question relates to the extent to which it may be possible to exhibit organisational equivalents of the components of EI. If so, how may these be developed at an organisational level?

These two questions are explored in more detail in the remainder of this chapter. It is important to point out that, while our work on individual EI has been rooted in structured empirical research, our proposals in this chapter are based on practical experiences, anecdotal examples and intuitive speculation (combined with some initial exploratory research). However, at this point in the book we sincerely hope that the reader has bought into the value of intuition in dealing with incomplete or ambiguous information!

3   Organisation Culture and Emotional Intelligence

The first question raised above takes us into the field of organisational culture. This is an extremely difficult area riddled with definitional and philosophical debate. It is exceedingly difficult to define exactly what is meant by organisational culture but this is at odds with our everyday experience. Most of us are able to recognise the distinct characteristics or 'feel' of the organisations in which we work or those that we deal with on a regular basis. These distinctive components are related more closely to the specific organisation than the business sector in which it operates.

For the purposes of this chapter we are less concerned with definitional niceties than we are with organisational realities. For our exploration we are proud to borrow the definition of organisational culture employed by the Chief Executive of a financial services organisation with which we worked: 'Culture is about the way we do things around here.' (In turn we believe that he borrowed this from Edgar Schein [1992]!)

3.1 A Framework for Considering Organisation Culture

While we may applaud the insight and pragmatism of the above statement, it is necessary to have a more structured framework within which to explore our question. The framework presented in *The Character of a Corporation*, by Rob Goffee of London Business School and Gareth Jones, formerly of Henley Management College, seems to present an extremely useful one within which we might explore our first question. Goffee and Jones (1998) explain that their framework relates to the social architecture of an organisation. From our perspective this provided a valuable link to our starting point in this chapter. The social architecture of an organisation is influenced by the perspective of the nature of organisations itself and, also, by the specific organisational evolution of their interpretation of this perspective in pursuit of their business goals. In addition, the Goffee and Jones model is appealing as it encompasses the following contextual elements:

1. There is no 'right' culture *per se*, only a culture that is appropriate to the business requirement.
2. Within an organisation differing cultures co-exist. They can do this effectively if each is appropriate to the respective needs of the business units, divisions or functions.
3. Culture is not fixed; it changes over time and, indeed, may be seen as following a life cycle.
4. While each cultural 'type' within the framework is valid in relation to specific business contexts, each can exist in a way that is positive and supportive or negative and damaging.

Having focused on the reasons for choosing the Goffee and Jones (1998) framework to explore our argument it is important to explain the nature of their cultural model. In essence, they demonstrate that the social architecture of an organisation may be seen in terms of two dimensions: sociability and solidarity. These dimensions are described in broad terms as follows:

3.1.1   Sociability

According to Goffee and Jones, sociability is about the level of friendliness among members of a community. It is to do with the extent to which relationships are valued for their own sake, and the extent to which people within the community relate to each other in a friendly, caring, way. Sociability is also impacted by the extent to which members of the community have shared values, views and ideas. This concept can be applied within business organisations as much as other communities. In an organisational context, sociability is also reflected in the degree of social links between the working and personal lives of the members of the organisation.

To an extent sociability displays a degree of persistency over time. Relationships which I form with others in my organisation are not instrumental (i.e., focused on results only) and relate to affectivity rather than results.

3.1.2   Solidarity

Goffee and Jones (1998) describe solidarity in terms of the extent to which there is commonality of tasks and a clear understanding of mutual interests. In a business context, solidarity is concerned with the extent to which members of the organisation have a clear and shared vision and related goals that are independent of the extent to which members like each other. The focus in high-solidarity organisations tends to be on results; there are clear goals, performance measures and a clear competitive strategy.

Unlike sociability, the solidarity dimension is more transient. Solidarity is contingent upon organisational goals and more intermittent. While the relationships in the sociability scale transcend changes in the organisational context, solidarity interactions do not. For example, today I work with you closely because the interaction between our two functions is crucial to achieving organisational goals. Tomorrow those goals change and our interaction no longer has any relevance. Thus, in solidarity terms, I no longer need to interact with you. This does not change my personal views about you as an individual. However, it does change the utility of our interaction in pursuit of core business goals.

In addition to defining the two dimensions Goffee and Jones (1998) point out that the resulting culture may be positive, in the sense of being appropriate for the business, or negative in terms of inhibiting the effective achievement of business goals. In addition, they highlight that there is no 'best' culture, only one that is appropriate for the needs of the business. The combination of these dimensions results in an overall model that is illustrated in Fig. 11.2. The four cultures emerging from this model may be summarised as follows:

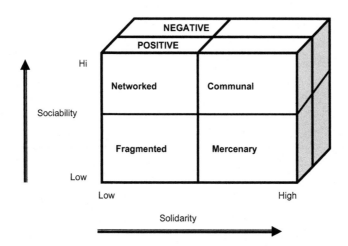

Fig. 11.2 Goffee and Jones cultural model. Source: Goffee and Jones (1998)

Networked Culture

The networked culture is one in which the level of sociability is high and the level of solidarity is relatively low. Thus, it is a culture, within which relationships are perceived as being more important than concentration on tasks and goals. Typically, it is a culture, in which results are achieved by tapping into and leveraging the relationship network.

Communal Culture

In an organisation with a communal culture there are high levels of both sociability and solidarity. Both relationships and tasks/goals are very important. Such a culture is typical of 'start up' operations where the founders and early employees are a community who value their relationships and are committed to a clear vision and goals for the business.

Mercenary Culture

The Mercenary Culture has an over-riding task and performance culture. Organisations with such a culture could be seen as being the corporate equivalent of 'driven' individuals. The focus is on winning; beating the competition.

Fragmented Culture

The fragmented culture is about the value to the business of individuality. Little is shared. Relationships are relatively unimportant and there is a low level of focus on shared goals and commitment to beating the competition. While this sounds negative, it can be appropriate for organisations which achieve performance by providing maximum freedom for individual innovation and are able to find opportunities to leverage such contribution. For example, a number of professional services firms operate successfully with such 'light' culture.

It is beyond the scope of this chapter to describe the Goffee and Jones (1998) model in detail (indeed the best way to access the detail is to read their own work). However, for the purposes of developing our ideas about the relationship between EI and organisational culture it is important to

Networked	Communal
Supportive of Emotional Intelligence	Supportive of Emotional Intelligence
Fragmented	**Mercenary**
Not Supportive of Emotional	Not Supportive of Emotional Intelligence

Fig. 11.3 Organisational culture and emotional intelligence

emphasise that each of the four culture types can have negative impacts on the organisation as well as positively benefiting a match between the culture and the business context. These negative effects arise when there is either too much solidarity or too much sociability to the extent that they damage the other dimension. Once again balance is important. For example, if a business needs a mercenary culture they can be over-focused on solidarity which, in turn, creates a potentially toxic interpersonal context.

Reflecting on this it is possible to hypothesise that some of these cultures would be more likely than others to nurture and promote EI. Fig. 11.3 illustrates the likely relationship between the organisation culture and EI.

Although the two dimensions provide a useful framework it is important to emphasise the appropriateness of culture. Goffee and Jones are now proposing that cultural appropriateness is related to the underlying strategic variables facing the business. This relationship is summarised in Fig. 11.4.

This view of the relationship between organisational culture and underlying strategic variables is somewhat simplistic. However, it is clear that the mercenary culture will be one in which there is a greater concern over the achievement of results than the interpersonal behaviours employed in arriving at goals. In a fragmented culture, relationships are incidental and not particularly valued. Thus in both of these cultures the environment will not be conducive to the development of the abilities that lead to high EI. This can lead to both voluntary and involuntary loss

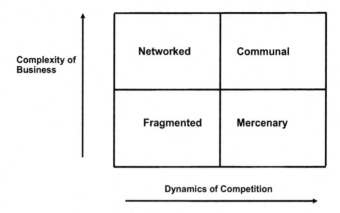

Fig. 11.4   Culture and strategic variables

of employees and potentially low morale. This would particularly be so if the culture were misaligned with the business requirements (i.e., negative mercenary or negative fragmented). In the high-sociability cultures (networked and communal) the value placed on relationships is such that the behaviours associated with high EI are likely to be endorsed and rewarded.

3.2   Emotional Intelligence Elements and Culture

Looking at the cultural relationship with EI is a useful point from which to explore the particular aspects or elements of EI that are described in Chapter 3. Indeed the model that we described in Chapter 4 provides us with a means of developing a more meaningful understanding of the relationship. For example, within a *mercenary culture*, not all elements of EI would be unrewarded. It is likely that, in such a culture, the element of intuitiveness would be highly valued and promoted. Influence could also play a role in terms of upward influence of those in clear power positions. However, the high-results focus of the culture could well lead to an 'ends justify the means' mind-set with resulting expediency in decision making and action. This would tend to lead to a low valuing and nurturing of the element conscientiousness. Using this approach to analysing the relationship between culture and the elements of EI enables us to

Table 11.1 Culture and components of emotional intelligence

Culture	EI elements		
	Likely to be rewarded/supported	Likely to be 'punished'	Neutral
Networked	• Interpersonal sensitivity • Conscientiousness • Influence • Self-awareness	• Motivation	• Intuitiveness • Emotional resilience
Communal	• Self-awareness • Conscientiousness • Interpersonal sensitivity • Intuitiveness • Influence		• Motivation • Emotional resilience
Mercenary	• Motivation • Emotional resilience • Intuitiveness • Influence	• Interpersonal sensitivity • Conscientiousness • Self-awareness	
Fragmented	• Intuitiveness • Motivation	• Conscientiousness • Interpersonal sensitivity • Self-awareness	• Emotional resilience • Influence

expand the model shown in Fig. 11.3 and develop a more useful framework. Table 11.1 summarises these expanded relationships. It was this way of looking at the links between the organisational culture and EI that became important to our development of the concept of an emotionally intelligent organisation that we explore later in this chapter.

From Table 11.1 we can see (using the driver, constrainer, enabler model) that:

- *Networked* cultures tend to support the enablers in the main, but discourage (or are neutral in relation to) the drivers.
- *Communal* organisations tend to value and promote a mixture of enablers, drivers and constrainers. They are unlikely to 'punish' exhibition of any of the components of EI. In this sense, they can be viewed as offering an environment that is broadly supportive of not only specific components but the balance that is the hallmark of high EI.

- *Mercenary* cultures are likely to primarily support the drivers of EI and, to an extent, the enablers. However, they tend to inhibit the constrainers.
- *Fragmented* cultures are more focused in their potential support for the drivers. Like the mercenary organisations they will be likely to inhibit the constrainers. However, they are more likely than mercenary cultures to also inhibit the development of the enablers.

4   Implications of the Cultural Impact on Emotional Intelligence

At this stage in our understanding of the relationship between organisational cultures and EI, it would be somewhat rash to be prescriptive in suggesting how organisations might react to an analysis such as has been presented above. However, two potential reactions might be considered. These are:

- Ensure that selection processes highlight the 'compatible and incompatible' elements of an individual's EI. Such data could either be used to screen out potential mismatches, or be used in an open discussion of realistic opportunities and challenges that might be faced by an individual who is 'mismatched' with the culture in this respect. While this approach may result in a loss of otherwise well-matched candidates, it could help to avoid the difficulties of losing people who find the cultural mismatch too uncomfortable and the potential of damage to morale of having such people remain in the organisation.
- Review the 'people systems' to identify potential areas for change that could reduce the EI punishing impact of the culture. This reaction, while potentially having a long-term impact on the nature of the culture may be attainable in a way which significant or fundamental culture change could not.
- If the organisation is completely comfortable with the fit between its culture and its business requirements, the first of these options may be the more appropriate. If there is any sense that the culture may need to

change in the mid- to long-term, or that there are undesirable negative elements of the culture present, the second option could be useful.

- Consideration of the impact of 'people' systems and processes on the support for, and development of, the EI of individuals is likely to entail examination of the following areas:

  - *Reward systems* Are results the only drivers of reward decisions? Would it be possible to include behaviours or 'softer' objectives (e.g., levels of employee satisfaction) in the reward decision criteria without damaging the business objectives being supported by the current system?

  - *Promotion systems* Do the current promotion systems include criteria that reflect elements of EI? Could the criteria be extended to include such elements (or more of them) without damage to the goals and success criteria of the system?

  - *Competency frameworks* If competency frameworks are employed within the organisation, do they include the elements of EI? If not, could these be added in a practical way without diluting the focus and purposes of the framework?

  - *Training and development systems* Are any of the elements of EI dealt with on company training programmes? If not, could they be included or covered in separate programmes? Do developmental processes (e.g., needs analysis, coaching) focus on behaviours as well as business/technical/professional topics? If not, could a shift in focus be effected in a practical way?

  - *Performance appraisal* Does the performance appraisal system encompass reviews of behaviours as well as results? If not, could the behavioural elements be included without detracting from the business goals of the organisation?

5 Can Organisations be Emotionally Intelligent?

In the preceding sections of this chapter we focused on the way in which organisational culture impacts on the climate in which individual EI is exercised and developed. In the context of our review of developing thoughts on leadership it is also important to recognise that the values of senior leaders play an important role in setting an organisational culture (as does their EI).

We now turn to the second question that we raised at the beginning of the chapter—can organisations be emotionally intelligent? While one aspect of an emotionally intelligent organisation would be the creation of a climate that fosters the development of individual EI, we suggest that the idea of an emotionally intelligent organisation is broader than this.

The resource-based view of strategy entails consideration of organisational competencies or capabilities. Our starting point for the examination of individual EI was individual competencies. The seven components of EI are, in themselves, competency based. There would seem to be a logic that lends some support, through a competency argument, for the concept of organisational EI. A way of developing a picture of what an emotionally intelligent organisation might be like is to identify the organisation level equivalents of the seven components of EI. Our proposed organisational components are summarised below.

Self-awareness: The organisation has processes in place that make it aware of how it feels about its business, products, markets and stakeholders at any time. This awareness is based on a clear self-image that is widely shared within the organisation. It is aware of how these feelings impact on its decisions and behaviours. It is aware of how stakeholders and other outsiders perceive the organisation and its actions.

Emotional resilience: The organisation has processes in place that enable it to absorb attack and criticism (particularly if it is perceived as unfair or unjust). It is able to manage internal communications in a way that ensures that such attacks do not deflect it from its strategy. It recognises potentially damaging shifts in its internal climate and has systems for controlling and managing these.

Motivation: There are clear, well-understood and shared long-term goals. Events that appear to threaten or deflect performance are responded to in a way that ensures that the long-term strategy remains intact. Actions that are short term are avoided if their benefits will damage achievement of long-term aims. Business setbacks are seen as problems to be managed rather than leading to the abandonment of long-term goals.

Interpersonal sensitivity: The organisation has established processes that enable it to understand the feelings, needs and motivations of its stakeholders. It uses this information to underpin its strategies, actions and decisions. Processes are established to manage relationships with all stakeholder groups.

Influence: Structures are in place to ensure that in interactions with all stakeholder groups the organisation is able to present persuasive arguments that will support the achievement of goals deemed to be aligned with the vision, values and business strategy.

Intuitiveness: Processes are in place to encourage individuals and teams to make decisions that are perceived as essential to business performance when faced with incomplete or ambiguous information. The extent to which the organisation values and supports the use of individual experience and intuition, based on this experience, in the decision-making process.

Conscientiousness: What the organisation says in public, its advertising, PR and espoused values are consistent with how people experience the organisation. In addition, the organisation's behaviour is perceived to be in line with the prevailing ethical behaviour that society expects.

Using this framework, is it possible to position organisations in terms of their organisational EI? We believe that it is and have decided to use our knowledge (which is based on publicly available data) to present some illustrations of organisations that may be seen at the extremes on each of the scales of EI. Clearly, we are not in a position to suggest that there is clear evidence for this positioning—we are just offering some possible examples. Business changes rapidly and there is always a danger of being overtaken by such changes when writing about organisations. The examples we have selected are based on a mix of the organisation with contexts from the late1980s to early 2015. The summary of our initial viewpoint is shown in Table 11.2. While we accept that this is far from complete or robust it does, we believe, demonstrate the complexity of EI and the challenges of building an emotionally intelligent organisation. While our examples demonstrate a range of 'high and lows' on the organisational profile in relation to the components of EI (for example, we would see The Body Shop as high on self-awareness, motivation, influence and conscientiousness) we can see the same organisations as

Table 11.2 Organisations and emotional intelligence

Emotional intelligence factor	High EI	Low EI
Self-awareness	• The Body Shop • Virgin • Wrigleys	• Microsoft • UK banking Sector • Lehman brothers • Google
Emotional Resilience	• Virgin • Ryan Air • Marks & Spencer	• Shell • The Body Shop
Motivation	• Wrigleys • Ryan Air • Virgin	• European financial sector
Interpersonal Sensitivity	• Virgin • The Body Shop	• Microsoft • Marks & Spencer • Thomas Cook
Intuitiveness	• Virgin • Monsanto	• European financial sector
Influence	• British Airways • Virgin • The Body Shop	• Monsanto
Conscientiousness	• The Body Shop • Virgin	• Maxwell Communications • Polly Peck • Lehman Brothers • European financial sector

low on other components (emotional resilience and intuitiveness). At this point we would declare that this (without further evidence) is unfair to a single organisation (e.g., our illustration of The Body Shop). However, we believe it illustrates the principle in a way in which we can experience and understand organisations as an outsider. Similarly those that appear as organisations with high EI seem to score well across many scales and thus demonstrate *balance* (e.g., Virgin and The Body Shop).

The 'evidence' on which we base our attribution is that which is in the public arena and is summarised very briefly below. However, we are aware of how rapidly the interpretation of public data can be turned on its head. For example, the collapse of Enron in 2002 has totally repositioned our thinking about a number of businesses. In reading these examples, please reflect on the context of the perceptions of the organisation at that time.

Some of these examples are explored in a little more detail below.

Self-awareness: Both the ethical trading policies and focus on ethical development of pharmaceuticals figured highly in the development of The Body Shop. Many of their actions, advertising campaigns and public statements tended to highlight their acute awareness of how they *felt* about the reactions of others to their decisions and to disclose the underlying importance of their feelings about their business. Similar comments may be made about the UK organisation Virgin and the chewing gum company Wrigleys. These organisations all appear to show a clear vision that has an emotional as well as business intent.

At the other extreme, the descriptions we read about the legal challenges in the US and Europe faced by Microsoft and in Europe faced by Google indicate a relatively low level of organisational self- awareness. Similarly, in the UK many banking organisations faced with regulatory mis-selling actions (e.g., PPI mis-selling) and other problems appear to demonstrate low levels of organisational self-awareness. In the USA the example of the collapse of Lehman Brothers is one of extremely low levels of self-awareness.

Emotional resilience: While The Body Shop could be seen as an organisation with high self-awareness (prior to changes in ownership) the way in which it was affected by a challenge to its image (as reported in the media) could indicate relatively low emotional resilience. Contrast this with the way in which Ryan Air responded to attacks on its somewhat controversial approach to business that illustrate relatively high levels of resilience. Shell, when facing attack in relation to a number of environmental issues has appeared to exhibit low levels of emotional resilience while Virgin, having ventured into the UK railways market and being sharply criticised, appears to exhibit high levels of resilience.

Motivation: In the context of EI, motivation is about 'long-termism' and persistence. Organisations such as Ryan Air, Virgin and Wrigleys have all provided illustrations of sticking to decisions that underpin long-term strategies and forge short-term opportunities for financial gains or savings. A classic example of this is the fact that Wrigleys continued to advertise their product in the UK during World War II despite the fact that the product was not available, and would not be available until the conclusion of the war. On the other hand, organisations with relatively low levels of motivation (in EI terms) will take the short-term gains at the potential expense of failing to achieve long-term goals or financial returns. It is difficult to provide specific organisational examples, but it is possible to see that many players in the financial sector fall into this category.

Interpersonal sensitivity: Organisations that appear to place a premium on understanding the feelings, needs and motivations of stakeholders include Virgin and The Body Shop. At the other end of the scale, we once again return to the legal challenges to Microsoft and Google that appear to be exacerbated by inattention to the interests of stakeholders; until recently, the decline in performance of Marks & Spencer, the retail chain, which appeared (until late 2005) to have failed to be sensitive to the management of all stakeholder needs. Low sensitivity is also indicated by the impact on Thomas Cook of the failure to consider the needs and feelings of its stakeholders in their response to the death of two children in one of their holiday hotels.

Intuitiveness: The link between the needs of stakeholders being balanced with the long- term aspirations of the business in the light of incomplete or ambiguous information characterise this element of organisational EI. Once again, Virgin provides an example of a high EI organisation on this factor. Their entry into the UK financial sector market in the early 2000s against a background of increasing regulation, competition and uncertainty with no clear parameters for determining success represents a clear example of EI intuitiveness. Similarly, Monsanto's decision to invest heavily in the area of genetically modified crops in the midst of scientific, political and social ambiguity provides another clear example of organisational intuitiveness in EI terms. The extent to which mergers of many organisations in the European financial sector have been hinted at, explored and ultimately abandoned illustrates a potential lack of intuitiveness in EI terms.

Influence: Virgin provides a clear example of the organisational ability to influence stakeholders involving brand image and investor support. Similarly, British Airways, in spite of long-term domestic and performance problems, has been able to demonstrate such levels of influence. In spite of media reports and attacks of interest groups, The Body Shop demonstrated abilities that match our description of EI influence. However, in the debate over genetically modified crops Monsanto appear to have relatively low levels of Influence.

Conscientiousness: This is, perhaps, the most difficult area in which to provide examples (particularly negative ones). Within the UK, high-profile examples of low levels of conscientiousness would be provided by organisations such as Polly Peck (the CEO was recently imprisoned for fraud) and Maxwell Communications that were surrounded by unethical (and indeed illegal) practices. Similar issues have arisen in the USA with Enron and Worldcom. More recently, we have seen numerous examples within the banking sector of clearly unethical behaviours (e.g., fixing of LIBOR and currency exchange rates, mis-selling of products). Organisations demonstrating high levels of conscientiousness include Virgin (who have demonstrated this in a public and high-profile way) and the US-based ice cream chain, Ben & Jerry's who contributed a percentage of all sales to charitable causes, a value that pervaded the organisation. From the comments above it is evident that the concept of EI has potential meaning and benefits for both individuals and organisations.

5.1   Implications

As an individual, the need to consider how the organisation in which we do, or may, work and will support or punish EI can be an important consideration in our own career planning. Based on an understanding of our

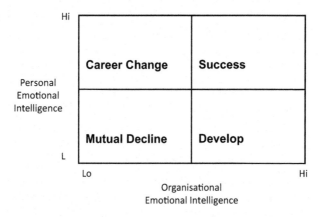

Fig. 11.5   Emotional intelligence: Personal/organisational fit

own EI, if we can identify the EI of the company we work for, or intend to work for, then we can identify a potential career strategy. Such choices are illustrated in Fig. 11.5.

If an individual has a high EI and works in a low EI company he/she should look elsewhere for career development. Alternatively, if an individual is in a high EI company, but has low personal EI then an attempt should be made to develop EI as this would be both supported and beneficial.

6   Research into Emotional Intelligent Cultures

The above review of the nature of organisational EI is, clearly, somewhat speculative. In general, the concept of organisational EI has not been the subject of much empirical research. In our own research we carried out a highly exploratory study using data from 16 organisations that had used the EIQ with a large number of their managers to examine the relationships between the average level of EI of employees and ratings of the organisation, using simple scales that we had developed to explore the 'cultural' dimensions of EI. This study produced indications that there was a relationship between these dimensions and average level of employee EI. This result prompted us to develop the idea further. Using the study results, together with a detailed review of the literature on organisational culture (in particular using the Goffee and Jones (1998) model) we developed a more structured cultural assessment questionnaire (the Emotional Intelligence Cultural Audit, or EICA).

The questionnaire contained 113 items that were rated using a Likert scale in the same manner as the EIQ. The statements in the EICA referred to the behaviours and processes that are observable within the organisation and that represent manifestations of the culture of an organisation. For example: *in performance appraisal discussions behaviours and results are given equal weight.* The questionnaire was developed to be completed by multiple respondents and to produce seven culture clusters designed to indicate the extent to which cultural manifestations support the individual elements of EI. These are the elements that are defined above.

Malcolm Higgs and Mary McGuire (2001) used this instrument in a study involving nine organisations and 164 participants. Multiple ratings of culture using the EICA were compared with average levels of individual EI (measured using the EIQ: M). Statistically significant relationships were found between all elements of EI and the cultural dimensions. Furthermore, the study showed that the EICA was a reliable instrument. In addition, the study provided some evidence to support the assertions we made above in terms of the relationship between EI and culture in relation to the Goffee and Jones (1998) culture model.

The questionnaire developed by McGuire and Higgs (2001) was found to be somewhat lengthy and in an extension of this work Da Camara, Dulewicz, and Higgs (2015) developed a new organisational EI questionnaire with 21 items (OEIQ-21). Da Camara (2015), in a study of 495 employees in the private, public and not-for-profit sectors (UK based), demonstrated that OEIQ-21 can positively influence corporate reputation (i.e., the emotional appeal or core reputation of the organisation) amongst employees. In addition, he found that the level of trust in senior management was related to OEI, and found a reduction in employee turnover intentions and increase in employee advocacy. Da Camara,

Dulewicz, and Higgs (2015) demonstrated that OEI has a positive influence on job satisfaction and organisational commitment that, in turn, acts to reduce employee turnover intentions (together these two attitudes explained 47 % of the variance in intention to leave).

Whilst empirical research into the concept of OEI is somewhat limited in volume, it is clear that it is a valid concept. Based on the research to date it does seem that it is important for organisations to develop and monitor their levels of OEI, and to be aware of the significance of organisational level factors in employee decisions to stay or leave. This does go against the popular idea that *'people don't leave organisations, they leave their managers'* because clearly there is a significant impact of organisational-level factors in employees decisions to stay or leave organisations. So, we can at least say that 'people do not only leave their managers, they ALSO leave their organisations'. Furthermore, OEI is a useful barometer of how employees feel about the organisation and its managers as a whole. Building on the earlier work on the OEIQ-21 a slightly longer version (the OEIQ-32)[2] has now been developed for use by organisations.

7   How Emotionally Intelligent is My Organisation?

Given that the concept of OEI has been found to be important, it is worth considering how emotionally intelligent your organisation is. As with individual EI[3] and LDQ,[4] it is best to do this using an established and valid questionnaire (in this case the OEIQ-32). However, in order to match ourselves to our organisation, we need a view on the EI of our organisation. A somewhat simplistic list of questions can prove to be a relatively useful guide; such a list is shown in Table 11.3.

The list in Table 11.3 is by no means comprehensive or a 'scientific' basis for evaluating the EI of an organisation. However, the more questions you answer positively from this list, the more likely you are to be in an organisation with high EI. This, in turn, helps you to make important personal and career development decisions.

Table 11.3 Checking organisational emotional intelligence

	High	Medium	Low
• Does the organisation have a clear vision?			
• Are there regular customer surveys?			
• Are there regular employee satisfaction surveys?			
• If the organisation is 'attacked' by the media, are responses quick and credible?			
• Do external 'attacks' deflect the organisation from its long-term plans?			
• Are decisions based on long-term goals or short-term/opportunistic profits?			
• Is a lot of effort put into internal communications?			
• If morale changes, does the organisation react quickly and appropriately?			
• Do all people have a clear view of the organisation's long-term goals?			
• Are all actions consistent with the organisation's stated vision, values and goals?			
• Are values clear?			
• Do you know how you are expected to behave?			
• Does the organisation invest effort in trying to understand the needs of all stakeholders?			
• Are you clear about who are the stakeholders?			
• Are decision-making processes clear and consistent?			
• Is there congruence between the stated position and values of the organisation and how it conducts its business?			

8   Developing Organisational Emotional Intelligence

The ideas and research that we have presented in this chapter indicate that climate or culture change programmes focused on the development of OEI would be an effective way of developing positive behaviours amongst employees that can maximise job satisfaction and organisational commitment and, in turn, lower turnover intentions in organisations. A climate or culture change programme focusing on the development of OEI could include the following objectives and activities based on the underlying dimensions of OEI:

- *Self-awareness*—ensuring that the organisation monitors and attends to the emotions and feelings of employees about all aspects of the business as well as ensuring that the organisation can identify and learn from its mistakes by encouraging employees and senior managers to discuss feelings about actions or decisions and reflect on behaviours.
- *Emotional resilience*—promoting a relaxed and trusting atmosphere in which managers and employees can discuss negative issues openly and engage in constructive criticism, which in turn increases the organisation's ability to absorb failures and recover from setbacks.
- *Motivation*—making the short-term and long-term direction and strategy of the organisation clear to all employees and communicating an attractive vision for the organisation in which employees understand how they can add value in their roles and contribute to success.
- *Interpersonal sensitivity*—supporting the development of interpersonal and/or 'soft skills' amongst managers and employees and prioritising the discussion of people issues when performance problems arise.
- *Influence*—allowing employees at all levels to influence the decision-making process and contribute their opinions, ideas and suggestions about how things should work. Also, developing a culture where senior managers welcome challenges to prevailing ideas and policies from employees lower down in the hierarchy.
- *Intuitiveness*—encouraging a flexible approach to work and decision making in which the role of intuition is valued and employees are given the freedom to take risks and follow their 'gut' instincts where necessary.
- *Conscientiousness*—ensuring that organisational behaviour, especially that of senior leaders, is in line with the espoused values and rhetoric of the organisation (i.e., 'walking the talk') and that integrity is rewarded amongst employees.

It is also important that organisations also support the development of the EI of its leaders and employees in order to optimise sustainable performance.

9 Conclusions

In looking at the leadership of organisations in today's uncertain, volatile, complex and ambiguous context we have argued for the development of emotionally intelligent leadership and a move away from the traditional 'heroic' model. We have pointed out that research indicates that leaders achieve performance for the organisation through establishing a climate and culture that engages and involves employees.

In this chapter, we have identified that an emotionally intelligent culture provides a clear basis for building employee commitment and engagement. While the model of an emotionally intelligent culture and related research is by no means exhaustive, we have hopefully, provided some 'food for thought'. Based on our work arrived at a useful definition of OEI:

Organisational emotional intelligence consists of organisational capabilities and competencies that facilitate the expression of individual emotional intelligence amongst employees and allow the organisation to be aware of the emotions of its members and to manage these effectively.

This definition and the areas covered in this chapter may prompt the reader to identify the 'people' systems and processes that could be reviewed in their organisation. Although not wishing to generate further lists to consider, we should point out that we chose the term 'people systems and processes' quite deliberately. The review process can go beyond the traditional HR or personnel processes. For example, the way in which meetings are organised and conducted can impact both positively and negatively on the support for and nurturing of EI. In any review within your own organisation it will be valuable to take a broad view of what you include in your interpretation of 'people systems and processes'.

Achieving a change in systems and processes intended to enhance the climate for the development of EI will take time and sustained effort. However, this mirrors, at an organisational level, the observation we made in Chapter 5 that developing individual EI takes time. For both individuals and organisations there are no 'quick fixes'.

Notes

1. For a good description of Weber's work see: Schils, E., & Finch, H. A. (2011). *Methodology of social sciences: Max Weber.* New Brunswick, NJ: Transaction Press.
2. The OEIQ-32 is available from VDA Assessment & Development Consultants.
3. The EIQ-Managerial is available from VDA Assessment & Development Consultants.
4. The LDQ assessment tool is available from VDA Assessment & Development Consultants.

Bibliography

Albrow, M. (1997). *Do organisations have feelings?* London: Routledge.

Collins, J., & Porras, J. I. (2005). *Built to last: Successful habits of visionary companies.* London: Random House Business Books.

Da Camara, N. (2015). Viewing the job-related and organisational antecedents of employee engagement through an emotional lens. Paper presented at *International Society for Research on Emotion (ISRE)*, Geneva, Switzerland, 7–10 July.

Da Camara, N., Dulewicz, V., & Higgs, M. (2015). Exploring the relationship between perceptions of organisational emotional intelligence and turnover intentions amongst employees: The mediating role of organisational commitment and job satisfaction. In C. E. J. Hartel, N. M. Ashkanasy, & W. J. Zerbe (Eds.), *Research on emotion in organizations: New ways of studying emotion in organizations* (Vol. 11). Bingley UK: Emerald.

Goffee, R., & Jones, G. (1998). *The character of a corporation.* New York: HarperCollins.

Higgs, M. J. (2009). The good, the bad and the ugly: Leadership and narcissism. *Journal of Change Management, 9,* 165–178.

Higgs, M. J., & McGuire, M. (2001). Emotional intelligence and culture: An exploration of the relationship between individual emotional intelligence and organisational culture. *Henley Working Paper Series, HWP 0113,* Henley Business School.

Schein, E. H. (1992). *Organisational culture and leadership* (2nd ed.). San Francisco, CA: Jossey-Bass.

12

Concluding Thoughts

1   Introduction

In this book, we have set out to explore the challenges of leadership in today's context of ever-increasing complexity, volatility, uncertainty and ambiguity. We have been conscious throughout that there is a vast literature that explores leadership, offers models and suggests solutions to the challenges of determining the nature and antecedents of effective leadership. In reviewing these in Chapter 6 we pointed out that the concept of 'heroic' leadership has dominated much of the thinking. We have also suggested that there is a demand for a simple answer that amounts to a search for the 'Holy Grail' of leadership. Organisations are all too often seeking relatively simple explanations and models that explain effective leadership. All too often, these 'silver bullets' fail to provide a basis for developing effective leadership. At the same time, the academic literature remains complicated and relatively inaccessible to practitioners. In reviewing the writing on leadership we determined from the outset that the context in which leaders find themselves today are not amenable to simple models and prescriptions for success. There is a real need, in our

© The Editor(s) (if applicable) and the Author(s) 2016   **223**
M. Higgs, V. Dulewicz, *Leading with Emotional Intelligence*,
DOI 10.1007/978-3-319-32637-5_12

view, for an approach to thinking about leadership that combines the rigour applied to academic research and the relevance desired by practice.

In our quest to avoid producing yet another definitive view or model of effective leadership we have been guided by the work of Karl Weick (1995) and were strongly influenced by his comment that:

We are not going to discover anything new. We need to use our knowledge to make sense in the context in which we are operating. (p. 16)

Based on this we have explored the elements of today's context and considered how these relate to the leadership challenge. There is little doubt that the context in which organisations operate today has changed dramatically over the past few decades. In Chapter 7 we reviewed the key drivers and implications of these changes. In doing this, it is clear that a major issue facing most organisations is the challenge of implementing change successfully. Indeed, we have highlighted the large proportion of changes that fail to achieve their goals—commonly stated to be around 70 %. In thinking about the costs associated with programmes designed to implement change it is clear that a better way of working on change needs to be found. We have argued that research into change has shown that a major area that can impact change success is the behaviour of those leading the change. One significant research study (Higgs & Rowland, 2011) demonstrated the importance of leadership to change success and indicated that around 50 % of the variation in success was explained by leadership behaviours.

Building on these thoughts, we suggest that a framework for making sense of leadership in a rapidly changing context needs to link leadership behaviours and style to the change context.

2   Emotions in Organisations

One of the notable outcomes of the developments in the context, in which organisations currently work, has been an increasing awareness of the emotional aspects of work. The 'traditional' view of management and decision making in organisations as exclusively rational processes has been replaced with a recognition that people and relationships at work bring an emotional dimension to these activities. This has also become more significant as the changing values and expectations of people coming into the workplace have shifted. Recognising this has led organisations to place more focus on 'people issues'.

As this shift has emerged so also has the concept of EI. In Chapters 2–5 we have explored this development and considered its impact for leaders and leadership. In doing this we have looked at both research and practice. In particular, we have considered how research has demonstrated the impact of an individual's EI on a range of work-related outcomes that include performance, stress, future potential and well-being.

Whilst some see EI as being a critical component for organisations to focus on, we have been careful not to position it as a solution for everything. Many have proposed that EI is fundamental to leadership. Again, we have taken a view that it has a role to play in leadership, but in making sense of today's context we do need to take a broader view. We have suggested that leadership in a complex setting requires a balance of EI, cognitive abilities (IQ) and managerial competences (MQ).

3   People are the Problem

In reviewing the literature on change there is a commonly mentioned cause of change failure—people have a tendency to resist change and make implementation difficult. In other words, *people are the problem*! We have found that the challenges and issues of engaging people in organisations are highlighted in much of the writing on leadership and is increasingly becoming a focus amongst the HRM community. The expectations of people at work and the associated complexity of the environment can be seen as combining to underpin the movement in leadership thinking away from the 'heroic model' to a more engaging and facilitating one. In making this shift there is also a recognition that in today's context an important focus of effective leadership is to create the conditions that enable people to realise their potential and thus contribute more effectively to the development and performance of their organisation. Combining these thoughts with the growing significance of emotions in organisations led us to suggest that, in today's context, we can make sense of leadership by considering the idea of *emotionally intelligent leadership*.

4   Emotionally Intelligent Leadership

In Chapters 8 and 9, we have developed further, the idea of emotionally intelligent leadership, showing the research evidence that underpins the framework. We have argued that such leadership is dynamic and there is no fixed style, or approach, that covers all contexts. Indeed, in describing the model of emotionally intelligent leadership we demonstrate that distinctly different styles are required for different contexts of change. In the spirit of sensemaking it is important that leaders develop a capability to adapt their style and behaviours as their change context shifts. We have shown that EI can be developed (see Chapter 5). In the same way, in Chapter 9, we have indicated that emotionally intelligent leadership is also capable of being developed (ideally using the LDQ[1] as a means of initial assessment). In doing this we have provided some development guidelines and frameworks designed to help the readers reflect on, and plan to develop, their own emotionally intelligent leadership capability.

In relation to EI, and the broader concept of emotionally intelligent leadership, we have highlighted that feedback from others plays an essential role. Gaining feedback from others is, in itself, a step in the process of developing a more engaging and facilitating leadership style. It is one aspect of seeing leadership as a relational process.

To a significant extent, much of our work with organisations and underpinning research has focused on EI and emotionally intelligent leadership at the level of the individual. However, more recently we have begun the process of working with organisations at a team level. In Chapter 10 we discussed the concept of an emotionally intelligent team and extended this to consider emotionally intelligent leadership teams in Chapter 11. This is an area where practical experience is ahead of research, and could provide the basis for future research studies. What we do believe, however, is that it is still important to focus on the individual's development of the critical capabilities. Individual development should be implemented in parallel with working on team development processes designed to ensure that the strengths of the team are optimised, and the weaknesses mitigated, in order to provide effective and context related leadership from the senior leadership teams in the organisation.

In Chapter 6, when considering developments in leadership thinking, we pointed out that, increasingly, leadership effectiveness is seen to be related to the leader's ability to develop a culture or climate that encourages the engagement of all employees with the purpose of the organisation. We picked up on this in Chapter 11 in our considerations of the concept of an emotionally intelligent organisation. Whilst research into this concept is at a relatively early stage that that has been carried out offers some promising insights that demonstrate the potential value of the concept to organisations. Building on this research, we have offered some possibly useful guidelines that can help leaders to develop an emotionally intelligent culture in their organisations. Given the current thrust of leadership thinking in today's context, emotionally intelligent leaders do need to pay attention to the culture that exists in their organisations and the need for change to support the development of emotionally intelligent and engaged employees. In terms of assessing the culture of an organisation (an essential start point in the process of culture change) we have presented some practical guidelines and highlighted a research based assessment tool (the *OEIQ-32²*) that could be of value.

5   Applications of Emotionally Intelligent Leadership

Throughout this book, we have sought to identify and discuss the practical applications of the ideas, concepts and research that we have presented and discussed. In broad terms, the main applications that we have considered relate to individual, team and organisation development. However, it is worth mentioning some further applications that we have been asked to explore when working with organisations.

5.1   Selection of People

Our frameworks for examining EI and emotionally intelligent leadership have been essentially seen in a developmental context. In essence, our questions have been 'How can you measure and develop an individual's EI, or emotionally intelligent leadership in a business or organisational context?' The extension of this line of enquiry to personnel selection applications (particularly in selection for leadership roles) needs to be considered carefully. For example, before pursuing such a route any organisation would need to be sure that selecting 'high EQ' individuals would contribute to the sustainable achievement of their strategic goals.

The research and data available to date primarily examines differences in 'success' and 'performance' among individuals already in post. Further research would be necessary in order to establish the predictive validity (among new entrant populations) of EI, and emotionally intelligent leadership, measures. We do know that a number of organisations have begun this work and are now using both the EIQ[3] and LDQ as a part of a structured selection process.

At present, the understanding of EI and emotionally intelligent leadership (and their associated measurement) could contribute to a selection decision as part of a broad and robust process. For example, an assessment of EI could have a place in an assessment centre or be used for selection purposes, as one source of input (along with others). In this way the EIQ or LDQ data could be used by assessors, as a further source that could assist them in refining judgements against a number of target criteria. For internal assessment centres the use of the 360°[4 and 5] questionnaire will enhance the contribution of EIQ to such selection decisions. In the future a similar LDQ 360° questionnaire could also prove to be valuable in this context.

5.1.1   Assessment of Potential

Given the points we made in Chapters 3, 4 and 8, it is inevitable that the question arises 'do EI or emotionally intelligent leadership capabilities predict leadership potential?' To a significant extent, our answer to this question mirrors our answer to the above question on selection. In many ways, the identification of leadership potential represents an 'advanced selection' consideration. In our view, given the research evidence to date the level of an individual's EI in organisations that place value on these characteristics can be a helpful input to a process for identifying an individual's potential. Furthermore, it can be helpful to use the assessment of an individual's EI to formulate a development plan that, in the right organisational context, will assist them in realising their leadership potential (assessed against a broader range of criteria). In a similar vein we have shown that the LDQ has a clear relationship to leadership effectiveness and could therefore be seen as a predictor of future leadership potential.

Overall, we are conscious of the tendency of organisations to seek a simplistic or 'black box' means of ensuring that they pick the 'right' future leaders. However, such decisions are complex and capable of being informed by relatively sophisticated (albeit resource intensive) methods of assessment. One aspect of the complexity is, as discussed in Chapter 7, the importance of context. Therefore, organisations seeking to identify potential future leaders need to have a view on the future nature of the context in which they will be operating. The 'bad news' for organisations requiring a 'quick fix' solution to the potential identification issue is that neither EI, nor emotionally intelligent leadership, provide this. While we have found some evidence of links between EI and leadership potential (see Chapter 8), and between the LDQ and leadership potential, it is clear that further research is required to establish a definitive relationship. However, reviewing Chapters 3 and 8, it is evident that such research is likely to be fruitful.

5.2   Career Coaching

The core proposition that we have explored in relation to EI and careers in this book relates to the research that demonstrates that it is EQ (given an acceptable level of IQ) that distinguishes between success and average progression in an individual's chosen career or profession. However, as we pointed out in Chapter 11, some organisations are fertile ground for individuals with high EI, while others are not. Individuals need to reflect on the match between their EI and their perceptions of the EI Friendly or Supporting/EI Punishing characteristics of the organisation they are either working within or seeking to join.

We have also shown, in Chapter 4 that there is research that demonstrates a relationship between an individual's personal values priorities and their EI. What we do not know, as yet, is what types of career are best suited to individuals who have high levels of EI, and which should be avoided. However, some of our research has shown some interesting links to specific roles and associated profiles of those roles in EI teams (e.g., the studies referred to in Chapter 10). However, further research is needed to explore the role that EI can play in career guidance and discussion.

We have emphasised the value of coaching interventions in discussing the development of both EI and emotionally intelligent leadership. In a broader setting we can see that the use of the LDQ in career coaching could provide a helpful basis for discussing the development of an individual for a leadership career, as well as considering their likely appetite for such a career based on their understanding of the critical capabilities required.

Over the past decade or so, we have seen a relative explosion in the area of leadership coaching. Whilst we have discussed the application of the concepts of EI and emotionally intelligent leadership development being aided by coaching, we have not considered the extent to which leadership coaches need to understand, and possibly exhibit, emotionally intelligent leadership. This is a topic that invites further investigation and discussion.

Readers will no doubt be able to think of other areas of application within their organisations. Indeed, we hope that our book will prompt them to do so.

6   Further Research

The topic of leadership is an extremely wide one as we have hopefully shown. We have tried to underpin our discussions of EI and emotionally intelligent leadership with evidence from a range of research. However, in exploring emotionally intelligent leadership we are working in an emerging area. Indeed, throughout the book we have highlighted where we think that more evidence may be needed, in order to provide greater confidence in our conclusions and their applications. Some of the areas that we do think would be valuable ones for future research are:

6.1   Applications to Selection and Potential Assessment

As we mentioned in considering the applications of EI and emotionally intelligent leadership in the preceding section, there is a need to carry out further research in order to establish clear predictive validity for both constructs when applied in a selection arena.

6.2   Emotionally Intelligent Leadership and Coaching

Again, as mentioned above, there is a need to provide further evidence, based on research, in the coaching arena. A number of possible research avenues here include:

- The effectiveness of coaching interventions with individuals undertaking the development of EI or emotionally intelligent leadership.
- The nature and effectiveness of coaching interventions with leadership teams seeking to improve their team emotionally intelligent leadership.
- The relationship between the EI and/or emotionally intelligent leadership capabilities of coaches and their effectiveness as a leadership coach.

6.3   Feedback and Measures

In discussing the development of both EI and emotionally intelligent leadership we have emphasised the importance of feedback. One way of obtaining this is through the use of 360° feedback from a range of sources (although for leadership work the most important source is direct reports—the followers). In assessing and developing EI a validated 360° tool is available (*EIQ: M-360*) and this has been used in some of the research reported. Nevertheless, more studies using this would be helpful. In terms of emotionally intelligent leadership we have developed a 360° research tool (the *LDQ 360*). However, there is a need to review its application in development and its validity in more detail prior to wider application and publication.

Whilst some authors are seeking to develop a team measure of EI we have argued that this is not appropriate (see Chapter 10), given that EI is an individual level construct. We suggest that a developmental approach, as outlined and illustrated in Chapter 9, is more relevant. Perhaps there is a need for more case- and qualitative-based research to substantiate this view.

6.4   Organisational Emotional Intelligence

As we discussed in Chapter 11, the concept of an emotionally intelligent organisation is an emerging one. Early research has shown that a reliable measure of organisational EI provides reliable data and a degree of predictive validity (the *OEIQ-32*). Further research to provide additional evidence that underpins the use of this tool would be valuable.

6.5   Cross-Cultural Applications and Evidence

In discussing the context of leadership in today's organisations, we mentioned the trend towards increasing globalisation. Within the leadership literature there is a general debate around the application of leadership models and measures developed in western countries to different national cultures. There is still much debate on the topic, with studies to determine cross-cultural validity producing somewhat mixed and often contradictory results. However, given our assertion that today leadership needs to be seen in the context in which organisations operate, there is a need for research that looks at the cross-cultural applicability of the models of

EI and emotionally intelligent leadership and the related measures (e.g., EIQ and LDQ).

6.6 Emotionally Intelligent Leadership and Individual Values Priorities

Higgs and Litchenstein (2010) demonstrate that individual values priorities are clearly related to EI. There is a growing academic and practitioner interest in the role of individual values in an organisational context. In part, this can be seen to result from the collapse of a number of organisations and corporate scandals leading to issues concerning individual ethics. At the same time (in a related development) we have seen the emergence of the concepts of authentic and responsible leadership. These both emphasise individual values. Given that the concept of emotionally intelligent leadership emphasises leadership in context and contains a dimension of conscientiousness and integrity, it would be useful to conduct research that looks at individual values priorities and emotionally intelligent leadership dimensions.

The above represents a significant future research agenda. Hopefully, readers from an academic background, with an interest in leadership, will be prompted to develop some of these areas or identify other related ones of interest. We would be delighted to hear from such readers and most happy to collaborate.

7 Conclusions

In this book, we set out to explore the concept of emotionally intelligent leadership. In doing so we did not want to add yet another definitive model that would help to find the 'Holy Grail' of leadership. Rather we wanted to look at the concept as a framework for making sense of leadership in today's organisational context of volatility, uncertainty, complexity and ambiguity. We do hope that we have achieved this aim.

We began our own journey with our work on the concept of EI. In doing this we were aware that the topic, some 20 years after its emergence, remains a controversial one. While much of the new research data provided by ourselves, and others, reaffirms the significance of EI and its robustness as a concept, it has also served to raise further questions. What is now even clearer is that the concept of EI is well grounded. It is more than a repackaging of old ideas or a branch of 'new age' thinking. It has real implications for businesses and those who work within them. Furthermore, its emergence as an idea is timely in terms of the emergence of new models relating to businesses and their strategies (particularly in a global context). As with many new ideas in the business world, there is a tendency to overstate the case. What is known and proven, in relation to EI, represents an extension of decades of work designed to inform our understanding of the relationship between individual characteristics, success and work. What is claimed often exceeds what is known and can be proven. In our development of the concept of *emotionally intelligent leadership* we have tried to avoid exceeding what can be evidenced. If we do so we offer speculation and possibility rather than certainty.

In examining the concept of emotionally intelligent leadership we have placed what is known about EI within the framework of developing thinking about the nature of leadership and the antecedents of its effectiveness. In doing this we hope that we have presented arguments and ideas rooted in rigorous research and relevant to practice. We do hope that, by providing practical examples and frameworks for assessing and developing a range of elements associated with emotionally intelligent leadership, readers will be able to take something of practical value and application from this book.

Finally, we do hope that we have presented an exciting picture of the nature and potential of emotionally intelligent leadership and highlighted some interesting and challenging areas for future study that will ensure that the topic does not suffer the consequences of a 'flavour of the month' leadership model. We believe that the journey to understand and apply emotional intelligent leadership is far from complete. Indeed, while the past few years have built our understanding of the concept, we believe that there is much more to be explored and, furthermore, this offers an exciting prospect. We truly hope that, having read this book, you share our view and our excitement.

Notes

1. The LDQ is published by VDA Assessment & Development Consultants.
2. The OEIQ-32 is available from VDA Assessment & Development Consultants.
3. The EIQ-Managerial is available from VDA Assessment & Development Consultants.
4. The EIQ-M 360° is available from VDA Assessment & Development Consultants.
5. The 360° version of LDQ is available from VDA Assessment & Development Consultants.

Bibliography

Higgs, M. J., & Lichtenstein, S. (2010). Exploring the "Jingle Fallacy": A study of personality and values. *Journal of General Management, 12*(3), 38–52.

Higgs, M. J., & Rowland, D. (2011). What does it take to implement change successfully? A study of the behavior of successful change leaders. *Journal of Applied Behavioral Science, 47*(3), 309–335.

Weick, K. E. (1995). *Sensemaking in organisations.* Thousand Oaks, CA: Sage.

Appendix A: Sample LDQ Report

Leadership Dimensions Questionnaire

Report on: Pat Jones
SAMPLE REPORT
5 October 2015

© The Editor(s) (if applicable) and the Author(s) 2016
M. Higgs, V. Dulewicz, *Leading with Emotional Intelligence*,
DOI 10.1007/978-3-319-32637-5

Leadership Dimensions Questionnaire Report

Overview of Report Format

This report is based on Pat Jones's responses to the Leadership Dimensions Questionnaire. The structure of this report is as follows.

Introduction
An outline of the model of the LDQ dimensions and three leadership styles and broad suggestions on how to use the report for development are presented.

Section 1: Results on the 15 dimensions
This section describes Pat Jones's results from the LDQ. It highlights possible areas on which to focus his development. When analysing the data provided bear in mind that all scores have been compared with assessments from a large and highly able managerial population.

Section 2: The three styles of leadership and the relation to context
This section presents Pat Jones's score on the LDQ organisational context sub-scale, which measures the degree of change he perceives he is experiencing at work. This will help to identify which one of the three leadership styles presented is most applicable for him at present.

Section 3: Development planning for the 15 dimensions
This section provides some broad developmental guidelines.

Introduction

This report provides information based on Pat Jones's responses to the LDQ. Research studies have shown these dimensions of leadership provide some of the critical determinants of effective leadership and have also shown that the really important aspects of leadership relate broadly to emotional and social competencies, intellectual competencies and managerial competencies.

The 15 dimensions are classified, and presented, under four headings based on the authors' model of leadership which consists of:

- Personal enablers
- Inter-personal enablers
- Drivers
- Constrainer

The dimensions in this model are produced in an overall profile, which is then related to three different leadership styles:

- Goal-oriented leadership
- Involving leadership
- Engaging leadership

The styles are described and profiled in the report. No style is right or wrong *per se*. Each style is appropriate in a different context relating to the degree of change faced by the leader. The questionnaire also identifies the degree of change that Pat Jones perceives will be faced by his organisation.

In this report, Pat Jones's results are examined in relation to a reference group, comparing his responses to the distribution of results from a relevant sample of managers and senior officers, to determine objectively his leadership profile and its implications. It should be useful to examine the individual dimension results. This will help to identify which components of leadership he might wish to reinforce or develop, in order to enhance his overall performance in the context of his organisation's strategy and his current role, using a comparison of Pat Jones's leadership style to that indicated by his assessment of the context in which he is working.

We suggest beginning by reviewing Pat Jones's results on the 15 dimensions, each of which is defined in detail in italics. They appear in the next section.

Section 1: Results on the 15 leadership dimensions

Personal Enablers

- A. Critical Analysis and Judgement

Gathers relevant information from a wide range of sources in order to identify and then solve problems. Has a critical faculty that probes the facts, identifies advantages and disadvantages and discerns the shortcomings of ideas and proposals. Makes sound judgements and decisions based on reasonable assumptions and factual information, and is aware of the impact of any assumptions made.

On this dimension Pat Jones's self-assessment places him above average.

- B. Vision and Imagination

Imaginative and innovative in all aspects of own work. The capability to establish sound priorities for future work. To have a clear vision of the future direction of the organisation to meet business imperatives. Also, to foresee the impact of external and internal changes on one's vision that reflects implementation issues and business realities.

On this dimension Pat Jones's self-assessment places him above average.

- C. Strategic Perspective

Rises above the immediate situation and sees the wider issues and broader implications. Explores a wide range of relationships between factors and balances short and long-term considerations. Is aware of, and sensitive to, the impact of one's actions and decisions across the organisation. Identifies opportunities and threats from both within and outside. Is aware of, and sensitive to, stakeholders' needs, external developments and the implications of external factors on one's decisions and actions.

On this dimension Pat Jones's self-assessment places him above average.

* D. Managing Resources

Plans ahead, organises all resources and co-ordinates them efficiently and effectively. Establishes clear objectives. Converts long-term goals into action plans. Monitors and evaluates staff's work regularly and effectively, and gives them sensitive and honest feedback.
On this dimension Pat Jones's self-assessment places him below average.

* E. Self-awareness

The awareness of one's own feelings and the capability to recognise and manage these feelings in a way which one feels that one can control. This factor includes a degree of self-belief in one's capability to manage one's emotions and to control their impact in a work environment.
On this dimension Pat Jones's self-assessment places him below average.

* F. Emotional Resilience

The capability to perform consistently in a range of situations under pressure and to adapt behaviour appropriately. The capability to balance the needs of the situation and task with the needs and concerns of the individuals involved. The capability to retain focus on a course of action or need for results in the face of personal challenge or criticism.
On this dimension Pat Jones's self-assessment places him below average.

* G. Intuitiveness

The capability to arrive at clear decisions and drive their implementation when presented with incomplete or ambiguous information using both rational and 'emotional' or intuitive perceptions of key issues and implications.
Pat Jones's self-assessment on this dimension positions him in the average range.

Interpersonal Enablers

● H. Interpersonal Sensitivity

The capability to be aware of, and take account of, the needs and perceptions of others in arriving at decisions and proposing solutions to problems and challenges. The capability to build from this awareness and achieve the commitment of others to decisions and action ideas. The willingness to keep open one's thoughts on possible solutions to problems and to actively listen to, and reflect on, the reactions and inputs from others.

On this dimension Pat Jones's self-assessment places him above average.

● J. Influencing

The capability to persuade others to change their viewpoint based on the understanding of their position and the recognition of the need to listen to this perspective and provide a rationale for change.

On this dimension Pat Jones's self-assessment places him below average.

● K. Engaging Communication

A lively and enthusiastic communicator who engages others and wins their support. Clearly communicates one's instructions and vision to staff. Communications are tailored to the audience's interests and are focused. One's approach inspires staff and audiences. Adopts a style of communication that conveys approachability and accessibility.

On this dimension Pat Jones's self-assessment places him below average.

● L. Empowering

Knows one's direct report's strengths and weaknesses. Gives them autonomy and encourages them to take on personally challenging and demanding tasks. Encourages them to solve problems, produce innovative and practical ideas and proposals and develop their vision for their area of accountability as well as contributing to the formulation of a broader vision for the business. Encourages direct reports to employ a critical faculty and a broad perspective in all aspects of their work and to challenge existing practices, assumptions and policies.

Pat Jones's self-assessment on this dimension positions him in the average range.

- M. Developing

Believes that others have the potential to take on ever more demanding tasks, roles and accountabilities, and encourages them to do so. Ensures that direct reports have adequate support. Makes every effort to develop their competencies and invests time and effort in coaching them so that they can contribute effectively and develop themselves. Works with others and identifies new tasks and roles that will develop them. Believes that critical feedback and challenge are important.

On this dimension Pat Jones's self-assessment places him above average.

Drivers

- N. Motivation

The drive and energy to achieve clear results and make an impact and, also, to balance short- and long-term goals with a capability to pursue demanding goals in the face of rejection or questioning.

Pat Jones's self-assessment on this dimension positions him in the average range.

- P. Achieving

Willing to make decisions involving significant risk to gain a business or other advantage. Decisions are based on core business or organisational issues and their likely impact on success. Selects and exploits activities that result in the greatest benefits to one's part of the organisation that will increase its performance. Shows an unwavering determination to achieve objectives and implement decisions.

On this dimension Pat Jones's self-assessment places him above average.

Constrainer

- Q. Conscientiousness

The capability to display clear commitment to a course of action in the face of challenge and to match 'words and deeds' in encouraging others to support the chosen direction. The personal commitment to pursuing an ethical solution to a difficult business issue or problem.

Pat Jones's self-assessment on this dimension positions him in the average range.

To provide an overview of Pat Jones's results, a profile chart which plots his scores on the 15 Dimensions appears below.

Self-Assessment Profile Chart

Name: Pat Jones

Sten	1	2	3	4	5	6	7	8	9	10	Dimensions
Personal Enablers											
A	.	.	.	.	.	.	7	.	.	.	Critical Analysis & Judgement
B	.	.	.	.	.	.	.	.	9	.	Vision & Imagination
C	.	.	.	.	.	.	7	.	.	.	Strategic Perspective
D	.	.	.	4	.	.	.	.	.	.	Managing Resources
E	.	.	3	.	.	.	.	.	.	.	Self-awareness
F	.	.	.	4	.	.	.	.	.	.	Emotional Resilience
G	.	.	.	.	.	6	.	.	.	.	Intuitiveness
Inter-Personal Enablers											
H	.	.	.	.	.	.	7	.	.	.	Interpersonal Sensitivity
J	.	.	.	4	.	.	.	.	.	.	Influencing
K	.	.	3	.	.	.	.	.	.	.	Engaging Communication
L	.	.	.	.	.	6	.	.	.	.	Empowering
M	.	.	.	.	.	.	.	8	.	.	Developing
Drivers											
N	.	.	.	.	.	6	.	.	.	.	Motivation
P	.	.	.	.	.	.	7	.	.	.	Achieving
Constrainer											
Q	.	.	.	.	.	6	.	.	.	.	Conscientiousness
Sten%	2	5	8	15	20	20	15	8	5	2	

Source: Total Norm Group (n = 1009)

Section 2: The 3 Styles of Leadership & Relation to Context

Effective leadership is increasingly being seen in terms of a combination of:

1. personal characteristics that are required to enable an individual to engage in a leadership role in an effective manner;
2. a range of skills and behaviours that need to be in place to provide effective leadership
3. a range of styles related to the context in which leadership is exercised; and
4. a range of ways in which the leadership behaviours may be exercised in a way that matches the personal style of the individual leader.

In addition, it is quite widely accepted that leadership may be exhibited at many levels in an organisation. The next part of the LDQ report provides an indication of the leadership style Pat Jones is likely to exhibit based on his responses to the questionnaire. Three leadership styles are identified within the author's model:

1. *Engaging leadership:* A style based on a high level of empowerment and involvement appropriate in a *highly transformational context.* Such a style is focused on producing radical change with high levels of engagement and commitment.
2. *Goal-oriented leadership:* A style focused on delivering results within a *relatively stable context.* This is a leader-led style aligned to a stable organisation delivering clearly understood results.
3. *Involving leadership:* A style based on a transitional organisation which faces *significant, but not necessarily radical changes* in its business model or modus operandi.

Three profile charts appear on the following pages and present, in turn, Pat Jones's score in relation to the range of scores (indicated by the shaded bands) representing each of the three style profiles. ***According to his self-***

assessment, the leadership styles that Pat Jones is currently most closely fitted to are Involving and Goal-oriented.

Interpreting the Style Profiles

The Organisational Context questionnaire (LDQ Part 2) examines the degree and nature of change Pat Jones perceives that he faces in his role as a leader. The higher he scores, the greater the degree of volatility and change in the context in which he exercises leadership. The total score ranges from 21 to 105. Within this range there are three broad categories reflecting different contexts:

Relatively stable:	21–58
Significant change:	59–73
Transformational:	74–105

Pat Jones's own LDQ Context score is 84 , suggesting his organisation is in the Transformational range. It is facing significant and fundamental change with the underlying business models undergoing transformation. *An Engaging style would appear to be the most appropriate of the three.* He should, therefore, pay particular attention to the profile chart for that particular style. Examination of the descriptions of each of the dimensions can determine which may need developing or exploiting in order for him to be more effective for this style. When reflecting on his development needs he will find that the final section of this report provides a detailed review of his scores on all 15 dimensions and developmental issues. The other two style profiles are presented in case he is on the borderline of two different styles or contexts, or he feels that he might be required to adopt a different style in the foreseeable future.

Self-Assessment Profile Chart

for "Goal Oriented" Leadership Style

Name: Pat Jones

Sten	1	2	3	4	5	6	7	8	9	10	Dimensions
Personal Enablers											
A	.	.	.	.	.	.	7	.	.	.	Critical Analysis & Judgement
B	.	.	.	.	.	.	.	.	9	.	Vision & Imagination
C	.	.	.	.	.	.	7	.	.	.	Strategic Perspective
D	.	.	.	4	.	.	.	.	.	.	Managing Resources
E	.	.	3	.	.	.	.	.	.	.	Self-awareness
F	.	.	.	4	.	.	.	.	.	.	Emotional Resilience
G	.	.	.	.	.	6	.	.	.	.	Intuitiveness
Inter-Personal Enablers											
H	.	.	.	.	.	.	7	.	.	.	Interpersonal Sensitivity
J	.	.	.	4	.	.	.	.	.	.	Influencing
K	.	.	3	.	.	.	.	.	.	.	Engaging Communication
L	.	.	.	.	.	6	.	.	.	.	Empowering
M	.	.	.	.	.	.	.	8	.	.	Developing
Drivers											
N	.	.	.	.	.	6	.	.	.	.	Motivation
P	.	.	.	.	.	.	7	.	.	.	Achieving
Constrainer											
Q	.	.	.	.	.	6	.	.	.	.	Conscientiousness
Sten%	2	5	8	15	20	20	15	8	5	2	

Source: Total Norm Group ($n = 1009$)

Self-Assessment Profile Chart

for "Involving" Style of Leadership

Name: Pat Jones

Sten	1	2	3	4	5	6	7	8	9	10	Dimensions
Personal Enablers											
A	.	.	.	.	▓		7	.	.	.	Critical Analysis & Judgement
B	.	.	.	.	.	.	▓	.	9	.	Vision & Imagination
C	.	.	.	.	▓		7	.	.	.	Strategic Perspective
D	.	.	.	4	▓	.	.	.	.		Managing Resources
E	.	.	3	.	.	.	▓	▓	▓		Self-awareness
F	.	.	.	4	.	.	▓	▓	▓		Emotional Resilience
G	.	.	.	.	▓	6	.	.	.	.	Intuitiveness
Inter-Personal Enablers											
H	.	.	.	.	▓		7	.	.	.	Interpersonal Sensitivity
J	.	.	.	4	.	.	▓	▓	▓		Influencing
K	.	.	3	.	▓	.	.	.	.	.	Engaging Communication
L	.	.	.	.	▓	6	.	.	.	.	Empowering
M	.	.	.	.	▓	.	8	.	.		Developing
Drivers											
N	.	.	.	.	.	6	▓	▓	▓		Motivation
P	.	.	.	.	▓		7	.	.	.	Achieving
Constrainer											
Q	.	.	.	.	.	6	▓	▓	▓		Conscientiousness
Sten%	2	5	8	15	20	20	15	8	5	2	

Source: Total Norm Group (*n* = 1009)

Self-Assessment Profile Chart

for "Engaging" Style of Leadership

Name: Pat Jones

Sten	1	2	3	4	5	6	7	8	9	10	Dimensions
Personal Enablers											
A	.	.	.	.	▓	.	7	.	.	.	Critical Analysis & Judgement
B	.	.	.	.	▓	.	.	.	9	.	Vision & Imagination
C	.	.	.	.	▓	.	7	.	.	.	Strategic Perspective
D	▓	▓	▓	4	.	.	.	.	.	.	Managing Resources
E	.	.	3	.	.	.	▓	▓	▓	▓	Self-awareness
F	.	.	.	4	.	.	▓	▓	▓	▓	Emotional Resilience
G	.	.	.	.	.	6	▓	▓	▓	▓	Intuitiveness
Inter-Personal Enablers											
H	.	.	.	.	.	.	7	▓	▓	▓	Interpersonal Sensitivity
J	.	.	.	4	.	.	▓	▓	▓	▓	Influencing
K	.	.	3	.	.	.	▓	▓	▓	▓	Engaging Communication
L	.	.	.	.	.	6	▓	▓	▓	▓	Empowering
M	.	.	.	.	.	.	▓	8	.	▓	Developing
Drivers											
N	.	.	.	.	.	6	▓	▓	▓	▓	Motivation
P	.	.	.	.	▓	.	7	.	.	.	Achieving
Constrainer											
Q	.	.	.	.	.	6	▓	▓	▓	▓	Conscientiousness
Sten%	2	5	8	15	20	20	15	8	5	2	

Source: Total Norm Group ($n = 1009$)

Section 3: Development Planning for the 15 Dimensions

Having reviewed Pat Jones's style profiles and reflected on the leadership style(s) appropriate for his role and context the following overview of his scores on each of the 15 dimensions may be helpful in formulating a development plan.

The following analysis looks at Pat Jones's relative strengths and weaknesses on each of the 15 dimensions. However, in interpreting these it is necessary to consider their relevance to the profile required in his current context. In some cases, he may have a score that is *above* that required in his current context. If this is so, Pat Jones might well reflect on how he might adapt his behaviour to make it more appropriate. For example, if he is in a transformational context and has an above-average score on critical analysis and judgement, he may need to think of ways of working that reduce his own contribution and enable others to develop these capabilities. However, the comments under each dimension reflect possible development needs that may be appropriate if the context indicates that a higher score on this dimension is required for successful performance in the context in which he is currently, or expects to be, working. In addition, strengths that could be deployed further are highlighted. Furthermore, Pat Jones could gain even greater insights by talking to his work colleagues about their perceptions of his behaviour in a range of relevant situations.

Personal Enablers

* A. Critical Analysis and Judgement

Pat Jones's responses to the form suggest that his *critical analysis and judgement* is at a high level. Generally, he appears to identify and solve problems, has a critical faculty and makes sound judgements based on reasonable assumptions.

- B. Vision and Imagination

Pat Jones's responses indicate that *vision and imagination* are at a high level. Generally, he appears to be imaginative and innovative, to establish sound priorities for future work, to have a clear vision of the future direction of the organisation and to foresee the impact of external and internal changes on his vision which reflect business realities.

- C. Strategic Perspective

Pat Jones's responses suggest that his *strategic perspective* is at a high level. Generally, he appears to see the wider issues, to balance short and long-term considerations, to be sensitive to the impact of his actions, to identify opportunities and threats and to be sensitive to Stakeholders' needs and external developments.

- D. Managing Resources

Pat Jones's score in the area of *managing resources* is in the below-average range. In some situations, he tends *not* to plan ahead, to co-ordinate and organise all resources efficiently, to establish clear objectives, to evaluate his staff's work effectively, and give them sensitive and honest feedback.

- E. Self-awareness

Pat Jones's self-assessment for this dimension produces a relatively low score. This could indicate that he is not always aware of his feelings and emotions in work situations. If he wishes to develop this dimension, Pat Jones might find it helpful to reflect on specific situations in which he has felt in control of his feelings and emotions. In thinking about these situations he may be able to identify specific actions that were helpful. He could then apply these in future situations that arouse strong feelings and emotions.

Whilst Pat Jones's overall score is below average on *self-awareness*, he appears to have strengths in relation to functioning effectively when experiencing changing moods and understanding the reasons why he feels overwhelmed, which could be exploited.

- F. Emotional Resilience

On this scale Pat Jones's self-assessment indicates that he is in the lower range for the dimension. Such a score could indicate that he finds it difficult to perform consistently when under pressure. It might indicate that he can become frustrated by challenge or criticism and therefore find it difficult to continue to perform effectively in these circumstances. A helpful way of developing this, if he chooses to, is for him to attempt to depersonalise criticism and challenge, and view it as a challenge to the ideas, proposals, and so forth associated with the task rather than a personal attack. It can be useful for him to engage others in discussion to review the problem and task from different perspectives in order to find a successful way forward.

- G. Intuitiveness

Pat Jones's self-assessment on this dimension produces a result that is in the average range. Such a score could indicate that, while he can balance fact and intuition in decisions, there are some situations in which he is uncomfortable in making decisions unless he has full and unambiguous data available. It may be that there are situations in which he either lacks the confidence to use his own experience to close any gaps in information, or believes such intuitive behaviour would lead to an incorrect or bad decision. One useful way of further developing his capabilities in this area is for Pat Jones to reflect on past business decisions he has made. In doing so, he could try to identify the differences in the type of decision in which he felt it essential to have the full data, and then reflect on the extent to which the additional data changed the 'intuitive' decision. He may find that his own experience led to intuitive decisions that were close to the final ones. He could then try to apply the insight from these reflections to his future decisions.

Pat Jones's overall score on *intuitiveness* is in the average range but it could still be advantageous to develop himself in respect of adopting a broader approach to decisions (i.e., not basing them purely on logic and facts).

Interpersonal Enablers

- H. Interpersonal Sensitivity

On this scale Pat Jones's self-assessment indicates that he is highly sensitive to other people. Therefore, he is likely to engage others in problem-solving and decision-making. In dealing with others he is likely to listen carefully and acknowledge their uncertainties, needs, views and opinions. It may be useful for him to identify the behaviours that lead to this understanding and the capability to engage and involve others, and ensure that he applies them consistently in all work situations.

- J. Influencing

On this scale Pat Jones's self-assessment indicates that he is in the lower range. Such a score on this dimension could indicate that he may find it difficult to win others over to his point of view. He may be frustrated, on occasions, by his lack of success in persuading others to change their viewpoint or opinion on an issue. If he needs to develop his capability in this area, Pat Jones might attempt to understand the perspectives and needs of those he wishes to influence before presenting his case. In presenting the case or idea, he could try to do so in a way which takes account of others' alternative perspectives and shows how their needs might be met.

- K. Engaging Communication

Pat Jones's responses suggest that he does not always display *engaging communication*. In some situations, he tends *not* to communicate in a lively, engaging and enthusiastic way, to communicate his instructions and vision to staff clearly, to tailor his communications to his audience, to inspire staff and audiences, or to adopt a style which conveys approachability and accessibility.

Whilst Pat Jones's overall score is below average on *engaging communication*, he appears to have strengths in relation to appearing approachable to his staff and encouraging staff to communicate with him, which could be exploited. He might also consider putting more effort into building his capability in using his enthusiasm to engage an audience when speaking in public.

- L. Empowering

Pat Jones's responses indicate that some aspects of *empowering* are strengths. In some situations, he appears to know his direct report's strengths and weaknesses, to give them autonomy and to encourage them to take on challenging tasks, solve problems, produce innovative ideas, develop their vision, and employ a critical faculty and a broad perspective.

Whilst Pat Jones's overall score on *empowering* is in the average range, nevertheless he might like to work on exploiting strengths in relation to encouraging staff to present sensible proposals based on reasonable assumptions and factual information, involving staff in developing a vision of the future state of the organisation and encouraging staff to question their assumptions.

- M. Developing

Pat Jones's responses suggest that *developing* is at a high level. Generally, he appears to encourage his staff to take on ever more demanding tasks, to ensure that they have adequate support, to make every effort to develop their competencies, to spend time coaching them and to identify new tasks which will develop them.

Drivers

- N. Motivation

Pat Jones's self-assessment on this dimension produces a result that is in the average range. Such a score could indicate that his capability to maintain his focus on achieving a significant goal or result appears to vary from one situation to another. In some situations he may tend to focus on short-term goals and actions at the expense of clear long-term goals or aspirations. If Pat Jones needs to develop this dimension he might find it helpful to identify the motives that enable him to sustain long-term performance and build a strategy to apply this understanding to a wider range of situations.

Whilst Pat Jones's overall score on *motivation* is in the average range, nevertheless he might like to work on exploiting strengths in relation to setting high, stretching goals for himself and being willing to accept only average performance from his team.

- P. Achieving

Pat Jones's responses indicate that *achieving* is at a high level. Generally, he appears to be willing to make decisions involving significant risk to gain an advantage, to base decisions on core issues relating to success, to select and exploit those activities that result in the greatest benefits and to show an unwavering determination to achieve objectives and implement decisions.

Constrainer

- Q. Conscientiousness

On this scale Pat Jones's self-assessment indicates that he is in the average range. His self-assessment on this scale indicates that he may find that others occasionally perceive inconsistency between his words and his actions in practice. Developing consistency in behaviour may be helped by Pat Jones reflecting before acting and testing whether or not his proposed action is in line with what he has said to others about a task, situation or problem.

Whilst Pat Jones's overall score on *conscientiousness* is in the average range, nevertheless he might like to work on exploiting strengths in relation to adhering to prevailing ethical norms and dealing with only average personal performance.

Development Guidelines

It is possible to develop many aspects of Pat Jones's leadership style by planned and sustained development activities. Some dimensions are readily developable whereas others are more difficult to develop and it is more a matter of exploiting whatever capacity he may possess. If he wishes to develop his capabilities in line with the style(s) relevant to his needs, a useful initial framework follows.

Now:

- Reflect on, and identify, examples of behaviour that exhibited in different situations;
- Identify those dimensions that are seen as strengths in line with the style appropriate to the current situation and start to devise a plan to strengthen and build on these further.
- Identify those dimensions that are seen as development needs in line with the style appropriate to the current situation and start to devise a plan of possible behaviour changes that he could make to address these needs.

In his work:

- Consciously practise changing and reinforcing his behaviours and reflect on his responses to them.
- Continually seek feedback from colleagues on the dimensions he has attempted to change.

In Pat Jones's job, he will probably benefit from receiving feedback from others. He can then reflect on how they have perceived his reactions to significant events, challenges or decisions. He could also benefit from discussing his development actions and ideas with colleagues and, if possible, a mentor. This will enable him to obtain further advice and to 'fine tune' his proposed action plans.

Index

© The Editor(s) (if applicable) and the Author(s) 2016
M. Higgs, V. Dulewicz, *Leading with Emotional Intelligence*,
DOI 10.1007/978-3-319-32637-5

Printed by Printforce, the Netherlands